THE
Seed Bead
BOOK

THE
Seed Bead
BOOK

OVER 35 STEP-BY-STEP JEWELLERY PROJECTS

Kate Haxell

CICO BOOKS
London

For my mother, Jackie, whose impatience and inability
to sit still would make her a terrible beader, but who is
an inspiration in many other ways.

First published in 2005 by Cico Books Ltd
32 Great Sutton Street London EC1R 0NB

Text and designs copyright © 2005 Kate Haxell
Photographs copyright © 2005 Cico Books Ltd

10 9 8 7 6 5 4 3 2 1

A CIP catalogue record for this book is available from
the British Library.

ISBN 1 904991 20 3

Editor: Gillian Haslam
Designer: Janet James
Photographer: Matthew Dickens

Printed in China

Author's Acknowledgments

Much thanks to the lovely Luise, my right- (and left-) hand
woman on this project. Thanks to Cindy at Cico Books for
commissioning me in the first place. Gillian deserves all
credit (and extra gin) for structuring and editing the book,
while Janet, with her usual flair, made it look so good.
Thanks to Matthew for his always excellent photography
and to Amy and Elvis for lending us bits of themselves.
Thanks also to Philip for all the food.

CONTENTS

introduction

Beads are fascinating, beautiful, and very addictive. What starts out as the briefest of visits to a bead store can easily stretch into half a day, ending with a bag full of new (and unintended) purchases to be carried home and pored over at your leisure. This is very pleasurable, but the difficulty comes when someone asks you what you intend to actually do with all these beads. This book has over 35 different answers to that question—surely enough to satisfy anyone.

If you have recently fallen under the spell of beads, then you will find plenty here to teach and inspire you. The equipment and techniques sections starting on page 112 tell you all you need to know to get started. Beading isn't at all difficult and the step-by-step photographs and detailed instructions will guide you through the various weaving and wirework techniques that form the basis for the projects. You won't need much specialist equipment for any of the projects and the beads are relatively inexpensive—a small amount can go a very long way. Each project tells you what equipment and how many beads of which types you will need, and on page 114 you'll find a handy table that tells you how much that amount is in grams (the measure in which beads are usually sold).

There are some very simple projects, such as the Wrap-around Necklace (page 10) and the Chain Belt (page 94) that are perfect for the novice beader. Explore newly learned needle-weaving skills with the Lipstick Case (page 108), the Tassel Earrings (page 56), and the Fringed Choker (page 32). Take a step into wirework with the Snowflake Earrings (page 38) and customize favorite garments with Bead-embroidered Motifs (page 76). Each and every project builds on what you have learned in the Techniques section and shows you how to use it in a different way.

If, on the other hand, you are already a dedicated beader with a horde of bead treasures, you will find some original and contemporary ideas for jewelry and accessories, many of which can be made using your own favorite colors and types of bead. Turn to the Charm Bracelet (page 42), the Bead-lace and Button Scarf (page 66), the Beaded Bag (page 84), or the Fringed Bracelet (page 60) and see where your beads take you.

Kate Haxell

jewelry

Create your own beaded
jewelry, whether it be a
stylish fringed bracelet,
a delicate ring, a glittering
corsage, or a romantic
tiara. From updated
classics to thoroughly
contemporary pieces,
this chapter has projects
to suit every taste.

wrap-around
necklace

Wonderfully simple to make, and easy and versatile to wear, this necklace can be made in any color combination and with any kind of bead that has a hole large enough to take the wire. If you want to use a different repeat pattern, work it out on graph paper with colored pencils before you start threading the beads onto the wire.

MATERIALS

approximately 335 size 9
    moss-green seed beads
approximately 85 size 8 flesh-pink
    seed beads
approximately 45 moss-green
    cube beads
3 green glass leaf beads
2 green glass ball beads
tape measure
0.018in (0.46mm) gauge bead-stringing wire
9 crimp beads
chain-nose pliers

TECHNIQUES

wirework, page 124

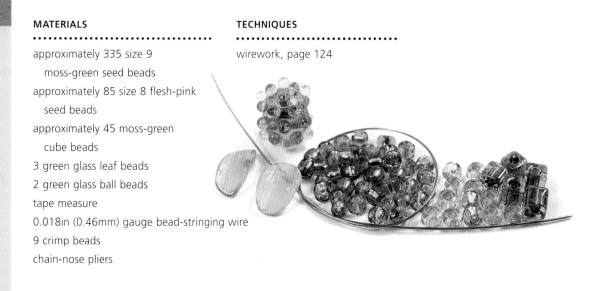

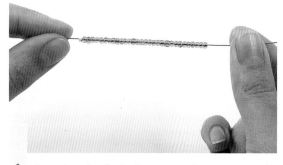

1 Cut a length of wire long enough to go around your neck twice, plus 10in (25cm). Thread on a crimp bead, followed by 30 green seed beads.

2 Push 1¼in (3cm) of one end of the wire back through the crimp bead and pull the loop of beads up tight. Using the pliers, squash the crimp bead.

3 Thread on a pattern repeat of seven green seed beads, one pink seed, one green cube, and one pink seed onto the long end of the wire. Bead enough wire in this sequence to go around your neck twice, then thread on seven green seed beads. When threading on the first beads, ensure that you slide them over the short end of the wire too, so that it is completely hidden.

4 Thread a crimp bead onto the beaded wire. Cut four lengths of wire, each between 3¼in (8cm) and 4¾in (12cm) long. Push the ends of the two longest lengths through the crimp and through several beads. Using the pliers, squash the crimp bead.

5 Thread one pattern repeat (see Step 3) onto one length of bare wire, then a crimp bead. Push one of the remaining lengths of wire through the crimp and several beads, then squash the crimp bead.

6 Thread two pattern repeats onto another length of bare wire, then repeat the process to attach the last length of wire.

7 Thread two pattern repeats onto the remaining length of bare wire. Thread on a crimp bead and then a leaf bead. Bend the wire sharply back on itself immediately above the hole in the leaf bead.

8 Thread the wire back through the crimp and several beads, ensuring that the leaf sits in the bend. Squash the crimp bead, then cut off the end of the wire where it emerges between the beads. Repeat the process on two more ends of wire, one from each branch, using one pattern repeat on one and two repeats on the other.

The necklace can be as sophisticated or as flamboyant as you wish it to be. The version shown below is made from matching size 10 and size 6 clear glass seed beads with a mauve core, and pale mauve fire-polished beads. The ends of the wire are simply crimped and cut short without additional decoration for a simple, elegant finish.

9 Repeat the process on the two remaining bare strands of wire, using the ball beads instead of the leaves. Thread one pattern repeat onto the wires, then seven green seed beads. Thread on a ball bead, then a green seed bead. Bend the wire above the seed bead, then back through the ball bead, crimp, and several beads, as before.

charm ring

This ring is a contemporary twist on a classic design. The black beads and silver charms used here are reminiscent of the traditional jet mounted in silver that was so popular in Victorian jewelry. However, colored beads can also be used to striking effect. Consider making a ring to match the Charm Bracelet project featured on page 42.

MATERIALS

approximately 70 2mm gunmetal
  hex beads
approximately 200 black
  delica beads
tape measure
beading needle
black beading thread
silver hanging leaf charm
6 5mm silver spacers
drilled dragonfly charm

TECHNIQUES

peyote stitch, page 116
simple fringe, page 121

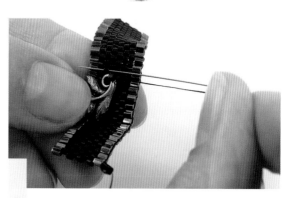

1 Pick up one hex, six delica, and one hex bead. Keeping the pattern of beads correct, work a strip of peyote stitch long enough to fit around your finger. End with an even-numbered row so that the two ends will lock together. Do not weave the long ends of thread into the beading.

2 Thread the needle with one long end of thread and weave it through to the middle of the strip to emerge through the second delica bead up from one edge. Pick up the leaf charm, then one delica bead, and take the needle back through the same bead in the strip. Position the delica bead so that it lies across the loop on the charm, hiding the thread.

3 Weave the needle through to emerge two delica beads above the first charm. Pick up two delica beads followed by one silver spacer, repeated three times, then two delica beads. Skipping the last bead, take the needle back through the string and back through the same delica bead in the strip.

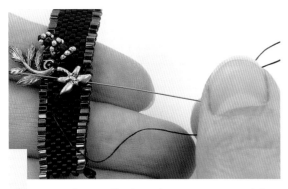

4 Weave the needle through to emerge two delica beads above the strand of fringe. Pick up the dragonfly charm, then take the needle back through an appropriate delica bead in the strip.

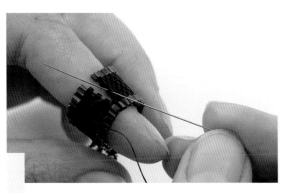

5 Join the ends of the peyote strip together using the remaining long end of thread.

GETTING IT RIGHT
....

When measuring your finger, remember to measure around the widest point, usually the second knuckle.

crystal corsage

Shimmering metallic beads and sparkling crystals are combined to make this glamorous flower. Pin it to a winter coat for instant color or to a classic little black dress for evening chic. The technique is simple, consisting of repetitions of the same action, so making the corsage is much easier than its good looks might lead you to imagine.

MATERIALS

30 pink fire-polished beads
60 orange fire-polished beads
30 pale green fire-polished beads
85 pink delica beads
135 orange delica beads
180 yellow delica beads
124in (310cm) 28-gauge silver
    wire
wire cutters
chain-nose pliers
3 velvet leaves with wire stems
narrow ribbon
brooch finding
sewing needle and thread

TECHNIQUES

wirework, page 124

1 Cut a 20-in (50-cm) length of wire and bend it in half. Thread on three pink delica beads, one pink fire-polished, and three pink delica, and slide them down the wire so the fire-polished bead sits in the bend.

2 Thread one pink delica bead, one pink fire-polished, one pink delica, one pink fire-polished, and one pink delica onto one end of the wire, sliding them down 2in (5cm). Thread the other end of the wire through these beads only.

3 Gently pull both ends of the wire until the beads sit snugly below those threaded on in Step 1. When the beads are in position, pull harder on the wire to tighten the loops.

4 Thread two pink delica onto each end of the wire and slide them down to sit next to the previous beads. Onto one end, thread one pink delica followed by one pink fire-polished, repeated three times, then one pink delica and slide them down 2in (5cm). Thread the other end of the wire through these last beads only, leaving the two pink delicas on each end free. Pull the ends of the wire as in Step 3, until the beads sit below the previous row.

Above: A close-up detail of one of the corsage petals, showing the neatly aligned rows of beads and the carefully graduated colors.

5 Thread two orange delica onto each end of the wire and slide them down. Onto one end, thread one orange delica followed by one orange fire-polished, repeated four times, then one orange delica. Thread the other end of the wire through and pull up tight, as before. Repeat this step twice more, using the same sequence of beads each time.

6 Thread two yellow delica onto each end of the wire, then one yellow delica followed by one green fire-polished, repeated three times, then one yellow delica. Thread the wire through and pull up, as before.

7 Make two more rows of green fire-polished beads, with two yellow delica on each end of the wire before both rows. The first row has two fire-polished beads, with a yellow delica before and after each one. The second row has one fire-polished bead, with a yellow delica either side. Repeat Steps 1–7 to make five petals in total.

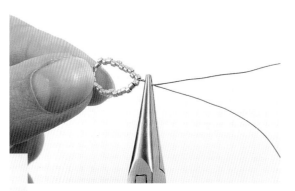

8 To make a cental stamen, cut an 8-in (20-cm) length of wire. Thread 25 yellow delica beads onto the center of the wire, then twist the ends of the wire together to form a loop.

9 Twist the loop around itself to form a helix. Make two more stamens the same way.

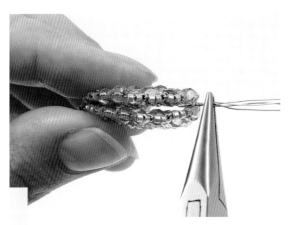

10 Hold two petals together and, using pliers, twist the ends of the wires tightly together so that the last yellow beads touch one another.

11 Add the rest of the petals, twisting their wires around those of the first two. Keep the petals as tightly together as possible.

12 Spread the petals out to form a flower. Slip each stamen into the center of the flower and twist its wire ends around those of the petals. Arrange them to fill the center of the flower.

13 Arrange the leaves around the flower and twist their stems around the wire ends of the petals.

14 Using cutters, cut the twisted wires to 2½in (6cm) long. Bind tightly over them with the ribbon, starting at the top, immediately below the flower. Secure the end of the ribbon by binding over it.

15 Bind down to the bottom of the wire, pulling the ribbon as tight as possible. Then bind back up the stem, binding in the brooch fastening securely as you go.

16 When you reach the base of the flower, trim off any excess ribbon and turn under the end. Push a pin through the stalk to hold the ribbon while you sew it in place with a few oversewing stitches.

variation

These delicate flowers are made using the same technique as the beaded corsage and can be used to decorate hair clasps, brooches, bags, and much more.

Each petal is made with pink 28-gauge wire and starts with three rows of pink delica beads with four, five, and seven beads on them respectively (there are no delica on the wire between the rows). Then there are three rows of orange delica—two rows of seven beads and one row of six beads. Finally, there are two rows of yellow delica—one row of five and one of four beads. The petals are wired together as for the corsage and the center filled with a single pale green crystal fastened in place with silver wire.

lace bracelet

Delicate in both style and coloring, this asymmetric bracelet looks intricate, but is actually surprisingly quick and easy to make. The narrow core band is needle-woven in peyote stitch and once you pick up the rhythm of the lace edging, you'll complete it at speed. Choose two colors of bead to complement a favorite outfit and in a couple of hours you can create a unique bracelet of your own.

MATERIALS

approximately 525 pale aqua
    delica beads
approximately 425 sea-green
    delica beads
tape measure
beading needle
green beading thread
silver clasp and ring

TECHNIQUES

peyote stitch, page 116
circles and loops, page 120
attaching findings, page 121

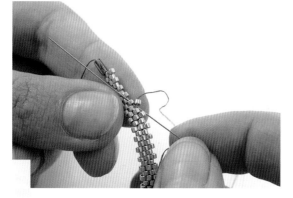

1 Measure your wrist, taking a snug measurement. Pick up enough aqua beads to make a string the measured length: the number of beads must be even and must be divisible by three. Work five rows of peyote stitch in aqua beads. Remove the stopper bead and weave in the ends of thread.

2 Thread the needle and weave it through to the end of the peyote band that is three beads wide. Bring it through one of the protruding edge beads, with the point of the needle toward the band.

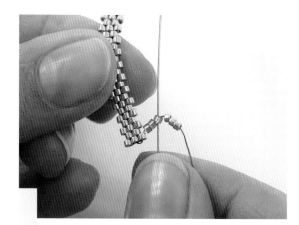

3 Pick up three green beads, then three aqua beads. Take the needle through the last green bead to form a circle.

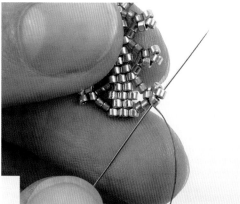

4 Pick up two green beads. Skip one protruding edge bead and take the needle through the next one along. Repeat Steps 3–4 until you reach the end of the peyote band. The last row—which is two beads wide—will be left bare. Repeat the process on the other edge of the bracelet so that both edges have a lace trim (see inset picture).

GETTING IT RIGHT
Keep the tension in the peyote stitch tight and even to produce a flat, straight band. When working the lace, keep the tension even, but not too tight, to produce a flexible lace edge.

5 Weave the needle through to the same end of the peyote band as in Step 2. On the first lace point, take the needle through the first two green beads and the first two aqua beads on the circle.

6 Pick up three green and three aqua beads. Take the needle through the last green bead to form a circle, as in Step 3. Pick up two green beads and take the needle through the second aqua bead on the next circle along the band. Repeat Steps 5–6 until you reach the last lace point. Weave in the ends of the thread.

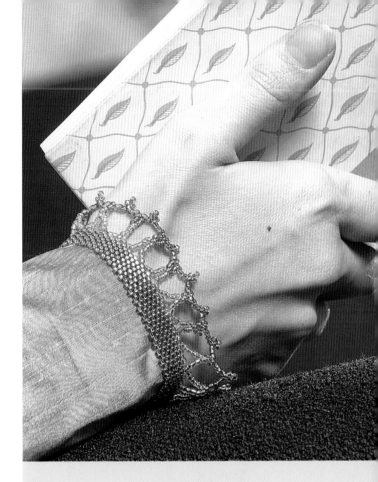

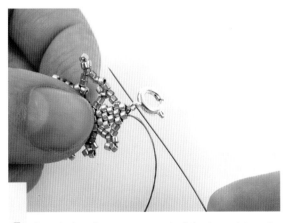

7 Attach the clasp to one end of the bracelet and the ring to the other end.

variation

Bead lace can also be used to trim the cuffs of an existing garment, giving it new glamour. This plain silk shirt was embellished with beaded cuffs worked using the lace pattern described in this Lace Bracelet, and size 11 pink and silver seed beads. The peyote band is 11 rows wide, with the first nine rows woven in pink beads and the last two in silver beads. Make the band long enough to fit comfortably around the fabric cuff. The first lace row is seven silver beads, three pink beads (to form the circle), then six silver beads. The second lace row is seven pink beads (the last three form the circle), then three pink beads. When you have finished the bead work, stitch the peyote band to the fabric, following the technique used to attach the peyote panel in the Compact Case on page 72.

fringed pendant

One of the great advantages of square stitch is that it allows you to incorporate beads of different types into a single piece of work with ease. In this project, bugle and seed beads are woven together, with swaying strands of two different fringes to add movement and sparkle to this unusual pendant design.

MATERIALS

183 size 12 pink seed beads
89 6mm blue bugle beads
pink beading thread
beading needle

TECHNIQUES

square stitch, page 119
simple fringe, page 121

1 Pick up 17 seed beads, one bugle, one seed, one bugle, and three seeds. Using square stitch and keeping the bead pattern correct, work eight rows, increasing by one bead at the end of row two and decreasing by one bead at the end of the last row.

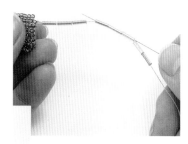

2 Weave the needle through to emerge through the end bead of the first full-length row. Pick up eight bugle beads and, skipping the last two beads, take the needle up through the string of beads and through the bead the thread came out of. Go down through the next bead and repeat the process on each of the six beads in the row.

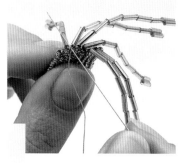

3 Take the needle through the stitch joining the beads at one end of the row.

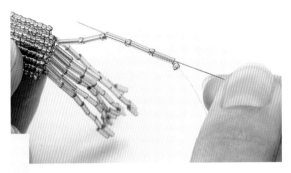

4 Pick up one bugle bead, then one seed bead, repeated five times. Skipping the last bead, take the needle up through the string of beads and through the stitch loop. Go through the next stitch loop along and repeat the process through each of the five stitch loops in the row.

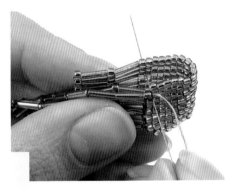

5 Stitch the fringed end of the strip to the back of the beaded piece, above the first row of bugles. Stitch between the last two rows of beads at the fringed end, and between the two rows of seed beads above the first row of bugles.

6 Make a string of beads long enough to go over your head. Slip on the pendant, then join the ends of the string.

brooch purse

The origin of this unusual brooch is unimpeachable—it's based on the classic amulet necklace purse. However, this design reinvents it, giving it a fresh, contemporary look and a new role in your collection of jewelry. These purses are decorative rather than practical, but they will hold some folded paper money, so you will always have your cab fare home at the end of an evening out.

Delica beads are ideal for needle-weaving in peyote stitch, as they sit snugly against one another to make a smooth, metallic beaded fabric. The delicate ruffle on the brooch band may look complicated, but it, too, is based on peyote stitch and is really very simple to work.

MATERIALS

· ·

616 gold delica beads
496 ice-blue delica beads
beading needle
gold beading thread
3/4in (2cm) brooch finding

TECHNIQUES

· ·

peyote stitch, page 116
simple fringe, page 121
attaching findings, page 121

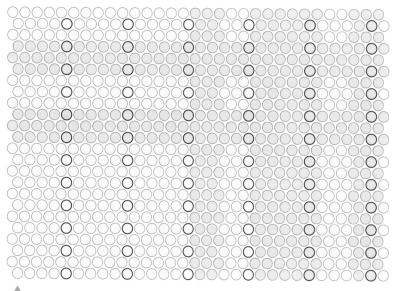

↑ First bead

Left: To follow this chart, start at the bottom left-hand corner and read the chart vertically (also refer to page 117). Every tenth row is shown circled in black to make the chart easier to follow.

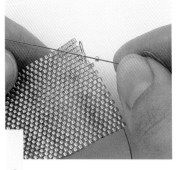

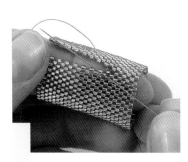

1 To make the purse, pick up three gold, three blue, three gold, three blue, and 12 gold delica beads. Following the chart on page 28, work the rectangle of peyote stitch.

2 Join the ends of the peyote rectangle to make a tube.

3 Fold the tube so that the ends of the narrow blue stripes align perfectly and join the bottom edge.

4 Work a simple fringe along the base of the purse. Attach a strand of fringe through the loop of each stitch joining the lowest row of the peyote on both sides of the purse. Make the front strand eight beads long and the back strand 12 beads long. Work a gold fringe from the gold sections of peyote and a blue fringe from the blue sections. Weave in the end of thread.

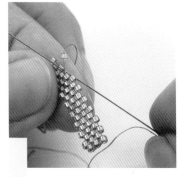

5 To make the brooch band, pick up nine gold beads, then three blue, three gold, and three blue beads. Keeping the stripe pattern correct, work six rows of peyote stitch.

6 Still keeping the pattern correct, work the first row of peyote ruffle. To do this, pick up two beads and take the needle through the next protruding bead on the peyote strip. Repeat to the end of the row.

7 Work the second row of ruffle by picking up two beads (in pattern) and taking the needle through the two beads added in the first ruffle row. Repeat to the end of the row. Weave in the end of thread.

8 To assemble the brooch purse, weave thread out to the blue edge bead above the ruffle on the brooch band of peyote. Thread on eight blue beads.

9 Take the needle through the top bead on the fold of the blue side of the purse. Go up through the next bead along in the same row, then back through the string of beads and pull it up tight. Weave the thread through the brooch band to the other edge and repeat the process with gold beads to join the purse to the band on the gold edge. Weave in the end of thread.

10 Position the brooch band centrally on the brooch finding. Stitch the band to the finding, stitching through the holes in the finding and through aligning beads in the band.

variation

This project can easily be adapted to make a traditional necklace-style amulet purse. Here, size 12 lilac seed beads and size 12 silver faceted beads have been used—the faceted finish gives the silver beads extra sparkle. Make the purse body, following Steps 1–4, but making the fringes 20 and 25 beads long. Weave a long thread up to the top bead on the fold on the lilac side of the purse and pick up a repeat pattern of 15 lilac and five silver beads, making a string long enough to go around your neck (remembering that the necklace must be able to go over your head, too). Take the thread through the opposite top bead on the fold and then take it back through the string and weave it into the body of the purse.

fringed choker

Movement always adds an extra dimension to beadwork, so rather than being just a flat band, this striking choker has an undulating fringed edge. Though the chart is large, beadwork grows quite rapidly on a loom and the fringing technique is simple, so the choker is actually fairly quick and very simple to make.

MATERIALS

approximately 575 size 12
   light amethyst seed beads
approximately 755 size 12
   dark amethyst seed beads
tape measure
beading loom
beading needle
purple beading thread
silver clasp

TECHNIQUES

loom weaving, page 122
simple fringing, page 121
attaching findings, page 121

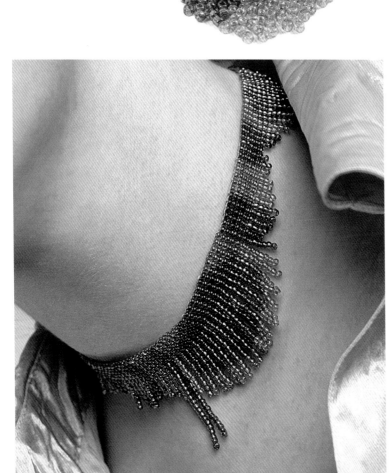

Right: To follow this chart, start at the top right-hand corner, picking up the bead marked with the arrow first.

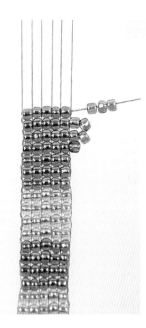

GETTING IT RIGHT

The chart produces a choker that measures 13in (33cm) long, with six rows equaling an approximate width of ½in (1cm). Take a snug measurement of your neck and subtract the length of the clasp you will use from this figure. If the resulting figure is more than 13in (33cm), add an equal number of extra rows onto each end of the chart to achieve the correct size, keeping the random stripe pattern so that they fit invisibly into the design. If your neck measures less than 13in (33cm), subtract an equal number of rows from each end of the chart.

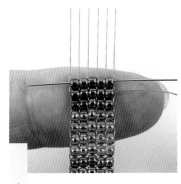

1 Set up the loom with six warp threads. Following the chart, weave the first 34 rows of the choker (see Getting It Right).

2 To make the fringed part of a row, weave the first five beads in the row as usual. Take the needle back through the row, taking it under the warp threads. (Don't be tempted to work the fringe straight out from the side of the band that the needle appears from once you have woven the five beads. If you do this, the band will not be "locked off" tightly and the choker will be loose and floppy.) Following the chart, pick up the number of fringe beads needed: these are circled in black.

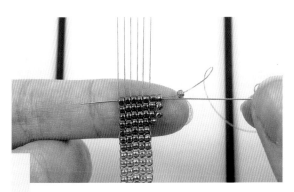

3 Skipping the last bead, take the needle back through the fringe beads and the row of five beads, taking it over the warp threads. Continue in this way until the chart is completed.

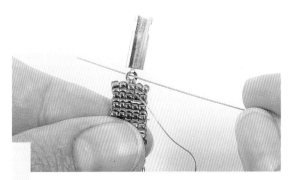

4 Take the finished choker off the loom and weave in the two outer ends of thread at each end of the choker. Using the two remaining central ends, attach the clasp.

bugle barrette

Densely beaded in vibrant turquoise and with a swinging "tassel" of fringe, this sparkling hair clasp is also easy and quick to make. Choose a color to suit your own hair, or to match a favorite outfit, and if you have long hair to be pinned up at the back, consider fringing right along the bottom edge of the strip of bugle beads.

MATERIALS

....

approximately 100 pale blue
   6mm bugle beads
approximately 280 size 10 pale
   blue seed beads
beading needle
pale blue beading thread
barrette finding
epoxy adhesive

TECHNIQUES

....

brick stitch, page 118
simple fringing, page 121

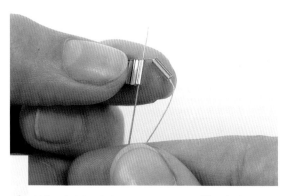

1 Using brick stitch, weave a strip of bugle beads that is two beads longer than the barrette finding.

2 Weave the needle through to emerge out of the last bead at one end of the strip.

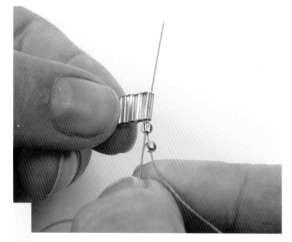

3 Pick up two seed beads and, skipping the last bead, take the needle back through the other seed bead and the bugle bead.

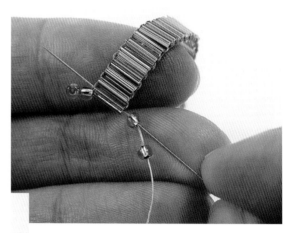

4 Repeat Step 3 at the other end of the bugle bead, but bring the needle out to one side of the first seed bead picot.

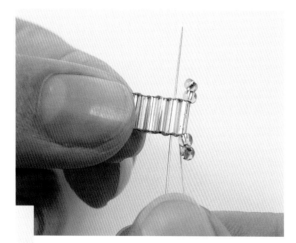

5 Take the needle down through the next bugle bead along in the strip. Repeat Steps 3–5 until ten beads remain without picots.

6 On the next bugle bead bring the needle out, as before. Pick up two seed beads, then two bugle, repeated five times, followed by two seed beads. Skipping the last bead, go back up through the string of beads and through the same bugle bead in the strip.

GETTING IT RIGHT

The strip of bugle beads must be neat and fairly firm or, when the picot edge is added, it will distort and not be flat enough to attach it to the barrette finding.

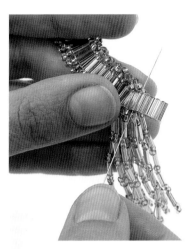

7 Make a picot at the other end of the bugle bead, as in Step 3. Go back down through the same bugle bead, bringing the needle out to one side of the string, and repeat Step 6 so that there are two strings of beads emerging from the bugle bead. Ensure that the needle emerges from the top of the bugle bead to one side of the picot.

8 Repeat Steps 6–7 on the next four bugle beads.

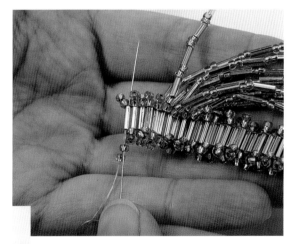

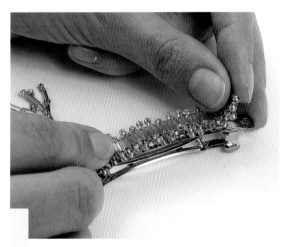

9 Make picots at each end of the last five beads following Steps 3–5.

10 Weave in the ends of thread. Spread a thin layer of epoxy adhesive over the back of the barrette finding. Carefully stick the beaded strip to the finding, positioning it centrally. Leave it to dry.

snowflake earrings

These glittering earrings are so simple in design, and so quick to make, that you'll want a pair in all your favorite colors—which isn't going to break the bank, as they require only a small number of beads each. The secret is to work methodically, threading each spike in turn and ensuring that it is in the right position before pulling the wire tight. If you have a pair of rhinestone stud earrings, make snowflakes to complement them, and to turn them instantly into glamorous evening jewelry.

MATERIALS

126 pink delica beads
36 pink fire-polished beads
2 pink cabochon stones
2 18-in (45-cm) lengths of
    28-gauge pink wire
2 stud earring findings with heads
    the same size or smaller than
    the cabochon stones
epoxy adhesive

TECHNIQUES

wirework, page 124

1 Bend one length of wire 2¾in (7cm) from one end. Slide a delica bead into the bend.

2 Slide one fire-polished bead, two delica, one fire-polished, and four delica onto the long end of the wire. Slide them up to the first delica, sliding them over the short end of the wire, too. Push the string of beads up tight against the top delica bead.

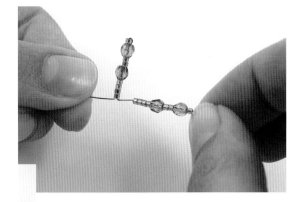

3 Bend the long section of the wire at right angles to the beaded spike. Slide on four delica beads, one fire-polished, two delica, one fire-polished, and one delica.

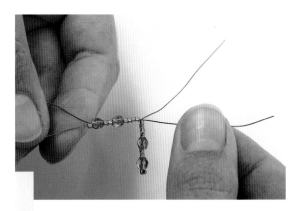

4 Skipping the last delica bead, thread the wire back through the string of beads and pull it tight. The lowest bead (the one threaded on first) must be tight against the base of the first beaded spike and there should be no gaps between the beads on the spike itself.

5 Repeat Steps 3–4 until you have made nine spikes in total.

6 Using pliers, twist the loose ends of wire tightly together. Cut them short and fold ends into the middle. Spread the spikes out evenly in a circle.

7 Lay the gems face-down on the work surface and spread a little epoxy adhesive onto the back of each one. Carefully lower the findings onto the gems, aligning the edges. Leave to dry.

8 Slip the bead snowflake over the finding post.

GETTING IT RIGHT

Instead of gluing gems to findings, use a pair of purchased stud earrings for the earring centers instead.

variation

These flower earrings are made using the same method, but with loops instead of spikes. Thread 21 size 12 pale pink seed beads onto silver wire, then take the wire through the first bead threaded on and pull the loop tight (see detail photograph, right). Make five loops, then finish off the wire and make the studs following Steps 6–8.

charm bracelet

A beaded version of a classic piece of jewelry, this charm bracelet can easily be customized to include personal favorite charms and other treasures. A single earring, the partner of which has long since vanished; a button from a christening dress; beads from a much-loved but broken necklace—all given a new lease of life by being incorporated into your charm bracelet.

MATERIALS

approximately 500 size 10 blue glass
   seed beads with a gold core
approximately 34 size 6 blue glass
   seed beads with a gold core
tape measure
beading needle
blue beading thread
bead loom
five freshwater pearls
silver clasp and ring
a selection of charms, beads,
   and "jewels"

TECHNIQUES

loom weaving, page 122
attaching findings, page 121

GETTING IT RIGHT

The secret to a successful charm bracelet is in the planning. Before you start, collect together as many charms and beads as possible and choose ones that complement each other. Once you have woven the bracelet, lay it flat and position the charms along it. Move them around until you are happy with the arrangement, then make a pencil diagram showing where each embellishment will go.

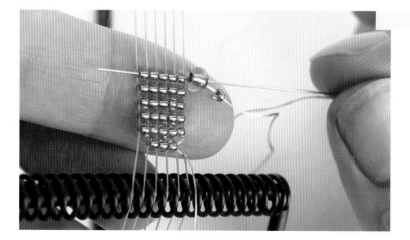

1 Measure your wrist, add 12in (30cm) to the measurement, and set up the loom with six strands of thread cut to this length. Weave one row of three beads and then five rows of five beads. On the end of the fifth row, make a picot by threading on one large bead, then a small one. Skipping the last bead, take the needle back through the large bead and the woven row.

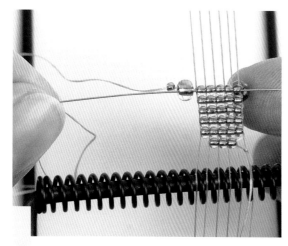

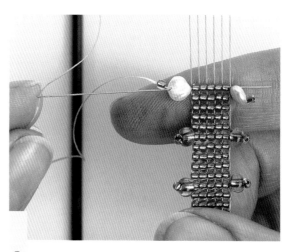

2 Repeat the picot on the other end of the row, passing the needle back through the woven row, but not through the first picot. Continue weaving the bracelet in this pattern: five woven rows with picots on the fifth one.

3 At a suitable point, make the picots with freshwater pearls and small beads.

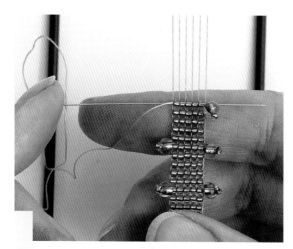

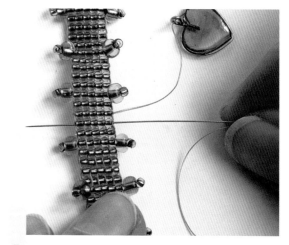

4 At a second suitable point, leave the picot off one side of the bracelet to make a space where you can attach a large charm. Continue weaving until the bracelet fits your wrist. After the last picot, weave four rows of five beads and one row of three beads. Weave in the outer two threads on each end of the bracelet and use the inner two to attach the clasp.

5 Weave thread in and out of several rows of beads to secure it. Bring the needle through the beads to the point where you want the first hanging charm to be attached. Take the needle through the charm, and then weave the thread through the beads to where you want to attach the next charm.

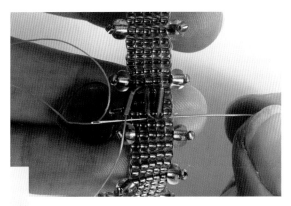

6 To attach decorative beads to the bracelet, weave the thread through the beads to the right place, as before. Bring the needle up between two beads, take it through the decorative bead and then back down through the beads in the bracelet. Here, three bugle beads have been attached.

7 Buttons, "jewels," beads, and hanging charms of all kinds can be attached to the bracelet using these two methods.

8 You can make your own hanging charms by threading on short strings of beads. Here, three freshwater pearls are sandwiched between glass seed beads using the simple fringe technique to make a charm.

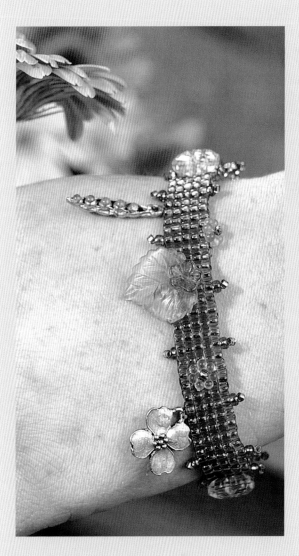

variation

Charm bracelets can be themed to complement the interests of the wearer. This pretty green and pink bracelet has been designed for a dedicated gardener and is decorated with an enameled flower and a peapod charm, plus glass flower and leaf beads. The band is made from size 9 green and pink seed beads, and the picots are topped with pink delica beads.

heart pin

The instructions for this pretty pin might look complicated, but once you start working the heart shape you will find them easy to follow, and there is also a chart to help you. You can work the heart in any color, but not in any bead—bugle beads and seed beads distort the proportions and will result in an oddly shaped heart.

MATERIALS

93 size 8 pale pink hex beads
32 rose pink delica beads
beading needle
pink beading thread
epoxy adhesive
stick pin finding

TECHNIQUES

square stitch, page 119

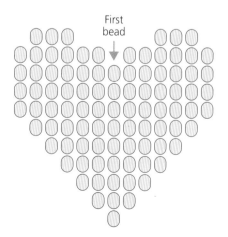

GETTING IT RIGHT

Making this heart does involve taking the needle through the bugle beads a number of times. If the beads become tight, don't force the needle through as you can crack the beads. Instead, choose a finer needle and thread to attach the delica beads.

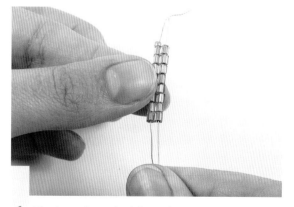

Above: To follow this chart in conjunction with the steps, pick up the bead indicated by the arrow first, then seven more. The ninth bead is added in Step 13. The steps take you out to the right-hand side of the heart first.

1 The heart is worked from the center out to one side, then from the center out to the other side. To start, thread the needle with 86in (220cm) of thread and, using square stitch, make a double row of eight beads. When you have added the beads, take the needle through both rows to stabilize them; do this on every row of the heart.

First bead

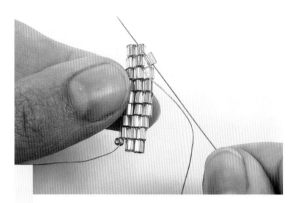

2 Increase by one bead at the end of the second row, and therefore by one bead at the beginning of the third row. Decrease by one bead at the end of this third row.

3 On the fourth row, decrease by one bead at the beginning and increase by one bead at the end (the increase will start the fifth row).

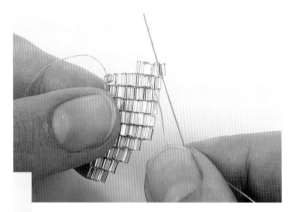

4 Decrease by one bead at the end of the fifth row (the row with the increase at the beginning), and by one bead at the beginning of the sixth row.

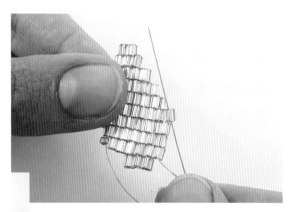

5 On the seventh row, decrease by one bead at the beginning and end.

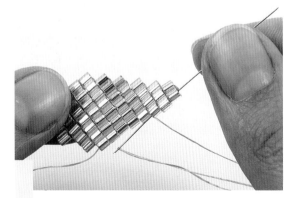

6 Remove the stopper bead and weave the thread through to the other end of the first row to start the other side of the heart.

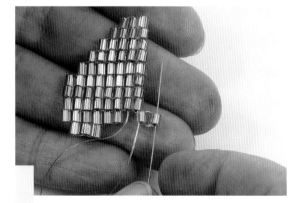

7 On the next row, increase by one bead at the end (the increase will start the next row).

8 On the next row (the row with the increase at the beginning), decrease by one bead at the end.

9 On the next row, decrease by one bead at the beginning and increase by one bead at the end (the increase will start the next row). Decrease by one bead at the end of this next row (the row with the increase at the beginning), and decrease again by one bead at the beginning of the following row.

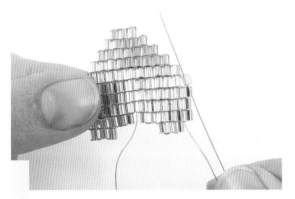

10 On the last row, decrease by one bead at the beginning and the end.

11 Using the same thread, pick up a delica and take the needle through the row of hex beads. Pick up another delica and take the needle back through the row, emerging to one side of the first delica.

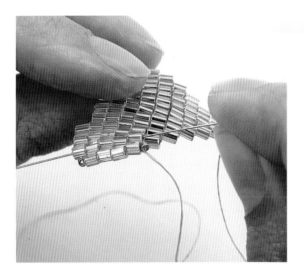

12 Take the needle down through the next row of stitched beads. If the next row is shorter, avoid any thread showing at the sides of the heart by taking the needle through the longer row starting at the bead adjacent to the end bead in the shorter row. Work this procedure in reverse if the next row is longer. Repeat Step 11 on every row of hex beads.

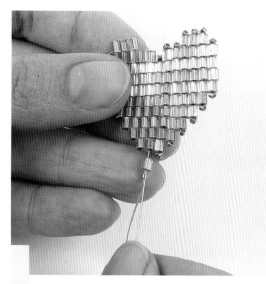

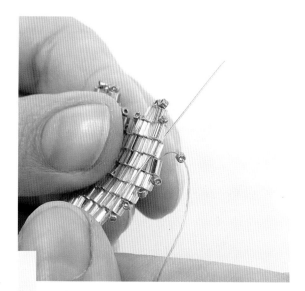

13 On the central row, add a hex, then a delica to give the heart a point at the bottom. Skipping the delica, take the needle back up through the hex and the rest of the row.

14 On the edge rows, bring the needle out between the first and second bead. Pick up a delica, then take the needle through the second hex to the next gap. Repeat the process to add a delica between each edge bead.

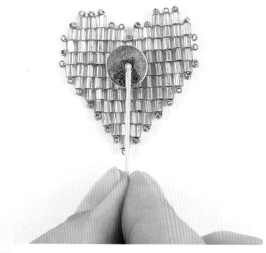

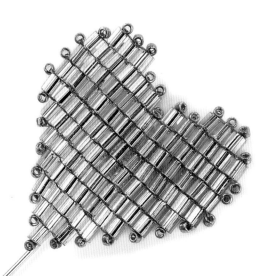

15 Using the epoxy adhesive, glue the stick pin finding to the back of the beaded heart.

This pendant is made in exactly the same way as the pin, but using size 10 hex beads to produce a smaller heart. The pale turquoise hex beads are edged with lime-green delica beads. Slip a jump ring through one of the top edge delica beads to to allow the heart to be suspended from a choker or chain (see step photograph, below).

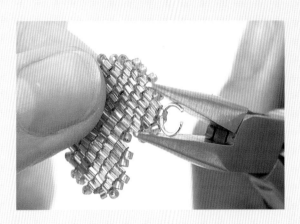

variation

Size 10 hex beads are also used to make this heart earring, which is edged with size 12 silver-gray seed beads. A stud earring finding is glued to the back of the heart with epoxy adhesive.

bead and pearl tiara

This delicately beaded tiara makes a perfect wedding day accessory and can be created in colors to match the bride's and bridesmaid's dresses. There are so many kinds of feature beads available and these, too, can be chosen to complement the wedding scheme. Alternatively, if made in vibrant colors with sparkling feature beads, this tiara would make a glamorous evening accessory.

MATERIALS

approximately 250 size 12 dark
    purple seed beads
18 purple fire-polished beads
8 purple glass flower beads
4 purple glass leaf beads
6 freshwater pearls
purple 28-gauge wire
metal tiara base
wire cutters
round-nosed pliers

TECHNIQUES

wirework, page 124

GETTING IT RIGHT

This is not a complex project, but it does take some time to bind the tiara base. It's worth doing this slowly and carefully as if it is badly bound, the whole tiara will suffer. Not only will the end result not look good, but the bound-in beads will move around and be difficult to add to.

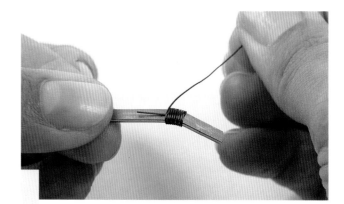

1 Cut 2 yards (2m) of wire off the spool. Bend the wire at right angles ½in (1cm) from one end and lay the bent wire against the inside of the tiara base, close to one end. Bind the wire around the base, binding over the bent end to secure it.

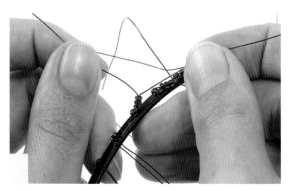

2   Continue binding the wire around 3¼in (8cm) of one side of the tiara base, binding tightly and evenly so that none of the base shows. Periodically push the wire down with your thumbnail to ensure that the coils are tightly butted up against one another. To join in a new piece of wire, use pliers to twist the ends of the old and new pieces tightly together against the inside of the tiara base. Cut the twisted end short, press it flat against the base and bind over it.

3   Thread 19 dark purple seed beads onto the wire. Continue binding, sliding a bead down the wire every ½in (1cm) to sit on top of the tiara base. Carry on binding tightly to hold it in place. Bind the final 3¼in (8cm) of bare tiara base without beads.

4   To secure the end, fold the wire ¾in (2cm) away from the tiara base. Wrap the folded end and the free end around the base in opposite directions, then twist the ends together on the inside, clip them short, and press them flat against the tiara.

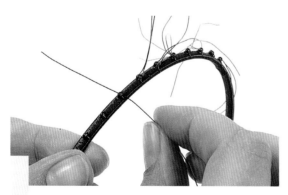

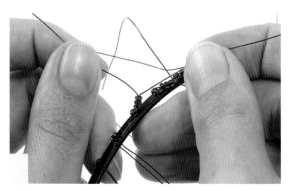

5   Cut 19 lengths of wire measuring 6in (15cm). Thread one length through each of the beads on the tiara base, pulling the wire halfway through, then folding it in half.

6   Thread three seed beads onto each length of folded wire, sliding the beads over both ends of the wire and down to sit against the bead on the base. Open the ends of the wire out to stop the beads falling off.

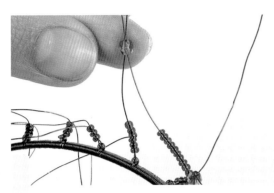

7 Take both ends of wire in the first group and one end from the second group. Thread them through a fire-polished bead, then open the ends out to stop the beads falling off. Thread nine seed beads onto the remaining wire from the second group and three beads onto one wire from the third group. Thread both ends through a fire-polished bead and open them out, as before.

8 Repeat the process across the tiara to the middle, varying the number of beads of the wires and occasionally threading on a pearl as well as some seed beads. Starting on the other side, repeat the process again, making the second side symmetrical to the first side.

9 When every end of wire has been joined to an adjacent one with a fire-polished bead, start adding the feature beads, working across one side of the tiara, then making the other side symmetrical. To add a flower, slip the flower bead over the ends of the wire and slide it down to sit on top of the fire-polished bead. Grip the wire with the tips of the round-nosed pliers just above the flower. With your other hand, wrap the wire tightly over one jaw of the pliers and then around itself between the pliers and the flower, forming a small loop. Wrap the wire around three times, then pull out the pliers and cut the end short.

10 Repeat the process with glass leaves on some groups of wires.

11 On occasional groups of wires, leave the fire-polished bead at the top. Make a wire loop as described in Step 9 to hold it in place.

tassel earrings

Though these earrings are not heavy, the fringing gives them a lovely swing. You can make the fringes as long or as short as you wish, though you may need to alter the depth of the brick-stitched section to balance the look of the tassel.

MATERIALS

234 size 12 iridescent mauve
 seed beads
126 6mm iridescent mauve
 bugle beads
beading needle
mauve beading thread
2 silver jump rings
2 silver loop earring findings

TECHNIQUES

brick stitch, page 118
peyote stitch, page 116
simple fringe, page 121

1 Pick up nine seed beads and, using brick stitch, weave seven rows.

2 Curl the brick stitch into a tiny tube so that the ends lock together and join them in the same way as peyote stitch.

3 Weave the needle through to emerge through the stitch loop between two beads on the bottom row.

4 Pick up one seed bead, then one bugle bead, repeated six times, then one more bugle bead. Skipping the last two bugle beads, take the needle back up through the string and the stitch loop.

5 Take the needle along to the next stitch loop and repeat Step 4 until each loop has a strand dangling from it—there will be nine strands in total.

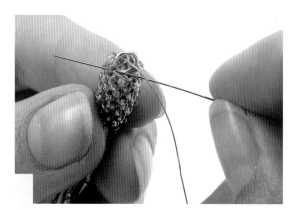

6 Weave the needle through so that it emerges through a bead in the top row of the brick stitch tube. Position a jump ring in the top of the tube and stitch it to the bead, stitching through several times. Repeat the process on the other side of the tube and ring.

7 Slip the jump ring onto the finding to complete the earring. Make another matching earring in the same way.

variation

Beaded tassels can be used to trim all sorts of jewelry and accessories, including a decorative beaded collar for a fabulously fashionable dog. The collar is woven in square stitch with a pattern of 11 matte pink seed beads followed by a leaf-green bugle bead, repeated to make a band the right length and five rows wide. The tassel is made in the same beads and attached to the collar with a string of three seed beads on either side (see step photograph, right).

fringed bracelet

This elegant and contemporary bracelet is deceptively simple to make, and although it is rather time consuming, once you get into the repetitive rhythm of the fringing, it grows far more quickly than you might imagine.

MATERIALS

approximately 350 size 10 silver
  seed beads
approximately 2700 size 12 silver
  metal seed beads
approximately 350 size 12 glass
  seed beads with a white core
approximately 700 size 12 gray
  seed beads
approximately 175 size 12 pearl
  seed beads

approximately 100 6mm silver
  bugle beads
approximately 45 2mm silver
  sequins
beading needle
gray beading thread
silver clasp and ring

TECHNIQUES

peyote stitch, page 116
attaching findings, page 121
simple fringe, page 121

1 Measure your wrist, taking a snug measurement. Pick up an even number of size-10 silver seed beads to make a string the measured length. Work seven rows of peyote stitch.

2 Attach the clasp to one end of the beaded strip and the ring to the other end.

3 Weave the needle through to emerge from an edge bead in one end of the peyote strip, with the point of the needle facing the finding.

4 Pick up 15 silver metal seed beads and, skipping the last bead, take the needle back through the string and through the bead in the strip.

5 Take the needle through the next bead along in the strip, again with the point of the needle facing the finding. Pick up 13 gray beads and make another fringe. Repeat the process with ten silver metal beads through the remaining beads in the end of the strip.

6 Weave the needle through to emerge from the edge bead in the next row of the peyote strip.

GETTING IT RIGHT

Apart from the bugle and the sequin fringes, make each fringe from a single type of bead. Balance the colors along the bracelet, making approximately 60 per cent of the fringes from silver metal beads, 15 per cent from gray beads, 5 per cent from white beads, 4 per cent from pearl beads, 12 per cent from silver beads and bugle beads, and 4 per cent from gray beads and sequins.

7 Make a bugle fringe, threading on two silver metal beads, then a bugle bead, repeated twice, and followed by two metal beads.

8 Make a fringe through every bead across the peyote strip, making each one between 10 and 15 seed beads long and balancing the colors (see Getting It Right, below left).

9 In the next row of fringing, make one of the fringes from sequins and beads. Thread on three gray beads, followed by a sequin, repeated three times, and followed by three beads.

10 Continue in this way, working a fringe through every single bead in the peyote strip until the whole length is fringed.

accessories

With a selection of must-have projects, such as retro-style make-up cases, a glamorous fringed stole, delightful dressing table accessories, and a slinky hip belt, you'll find plenty to make in this chapter.

bead-lace and button scarf

Crisp linen, sophisticated colors, and pretty bead lace combine to make this casually chic summer scarf. The weight of the beads gives it a lovely swing and the understated but detailed decoration makes it a perfect accessory for any smart party or summer wedding.

MATERIALS

approximately 5000 size 12 blue
   glass with pink core seed beads
beading needle
blue beading thread
2 20½-in (52-cm) lengths of
   ¼-in (5-mm) wide blue ribbon
   with pale green edge
59 x 20½-in (150 x 52-cm) piece
   of cream linen fabric
dressmaker's pins
sewing machine with zipper foot
cream sewing thread
sewing needle
selection of 40 small pearl buttons

TECHNIQUES

simple fringe, page 121

GETTING IT RIGHT

When working the beaded lace, don't pull the thread up too tight
or the lace will be stiff and you may pucker the ribbon.

1 Thread the needle and knot the end of the thread. Starting close to one end of the ribbon, make a few small stitches through the edge to emerge ¹/₂in (1cm) from the end. Pick up 17 beads, skip the last bead and take the needle through the next one, pulling the string of beads up tight.

2 Pick up nine beads. Take the needle through the sixth bead from the top on the previous strand.

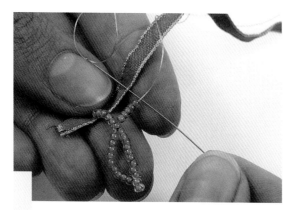

3 Pick up five beads. Take the needle through the edge of the ribbon ¹/₂in (1cm) from the previous strand.

4 Take the needle back through the last bead, then pick up nine beads.

5 Take the needle through the fifth bead below the intersect bead.

6 Pick up six beads. Skipping the last bead, take the needle through the next one. Repeat Steps 2–6 until 19¹/₂in (50cm) of ribbon has been edged with lace, ending with a Step 3.

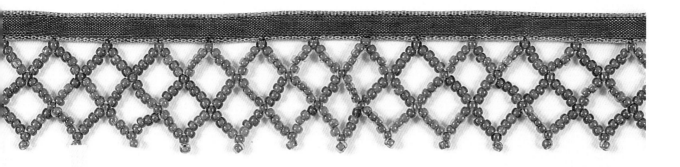

7 Edge the other piece of ribbon in exactly the same way, but if your ribbon is one-sided, ensure that the second piece is a mirror image of the first piece.

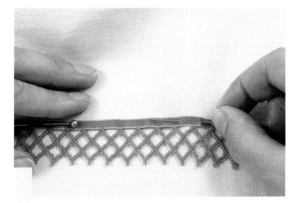

8 Pin a length of edged ribbon across each end of the scarf, 5in (13cm) from a short end, aligning the ends of the ribbon with the edges of the fabric.

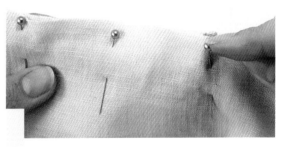

9 Right-sides facing, fold the fabric in half lengthwise. Check that the ends of the ribbons align perfectly and pin the edges of the fabric together.

10 Taking a ¹⁄₂in (1cm) seam, machine stitch across a short end and half way up the long open side, using the zipper foot so as not to catch the beads in the stitching. Repeat the process at the other end, leaving a 4in (10cm) gap in the long side.

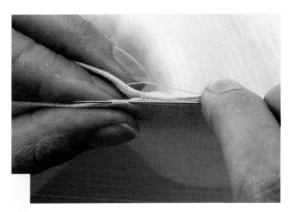

11 Turn the scarf right-side out and slip stitch the gap closed. Carefully press the seam, avoiding pressing the beads as they may break.

12 Arrange 10 buttons across the ribbon on one side of one end of the scarf, spacing them unevenly. When you are happy with the arrangement, mark the position of each button with a pin, pinning through all layers. Set the buttons aside in the order in which they were on the scarf.

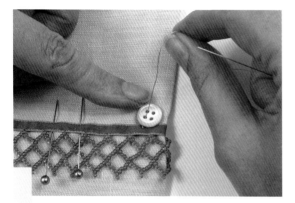

13 Thread the beading needle with blue beading thread and knot one end. Bring the needle up through the ribbon at the position of the first button and thread on the button.

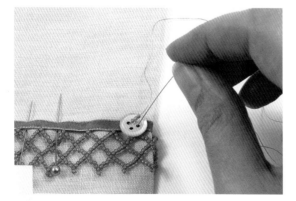

14 Pick up enough seed beads to span the gap between the holes in the button, then take the needle through the other hole and right through the scarf to the other side.

variation

The first strand of this fringe is five delica beads, one 4mm bugle bead, and one delica bead. Skipping the last bead, take the needle up through the bugle and one delica bead. Pick up four delica beads and take the needle through the edge of the velvet ribbon and then back through the last bead. Subsequent strands need only four delica beads before the bugle bead. The ribbon is attached to the silk fabric with bugle beads sewn on using straight stitch.

variation

This is a variation of the lace pattern used to make the Lace Bracelet on page 22. The same color of delica bead is used throughout and in both rows there are four beads before and after the circle.

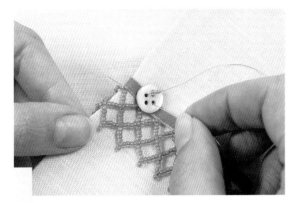 

15 Select another button similar in size to the first one, but not from those set aside in Step 12. Thread this onto the needle then thread on some seed beads, as before. Take the needle through another hole in the button to emerge through the corresponding hole in the first button on the other side of the scarf.

16 Take the needle through both buttons, and their beads, several times, then secure the thread around the base of the button with a firm knot. Repeat Steps 13–16 at each marked button point, then repeat Steps 12–16 on the beaded lace at the other end of the scarf.

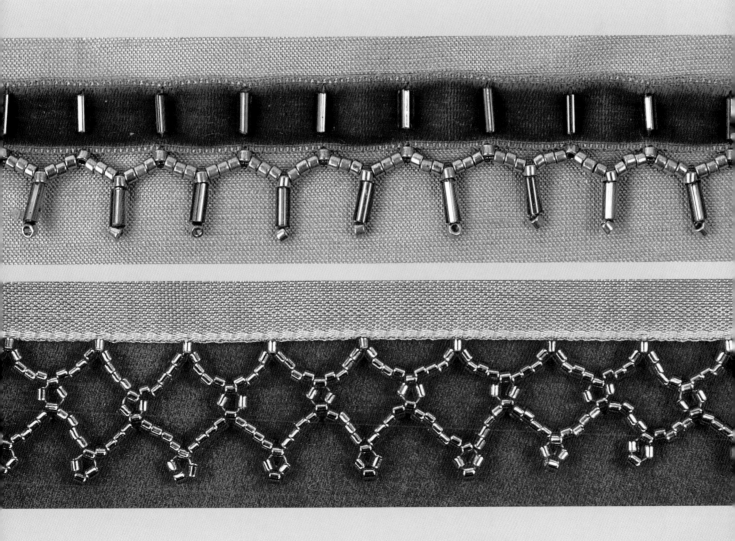

compact case

A contemporary twist on a classic accessory, this chic, felted wool case will turn a favorite, but rather battered, compact into a thing of beauty. Needing only the most basic sewing skills, it combines beading, sequins, and fabric in style.

MATERIALS

approximately 1100 size 12 pale
   gray seed beads
approximately 50 2mm silver
   sequins
beading needle
gray beading thread
4³/4 x 3-in (12 x 7.5-cm) rectangle
   of gray felted-wool fabric
dressmaker's pin

TECHNIQUES

peyote stitch, page 116
bead embroidery, page 125

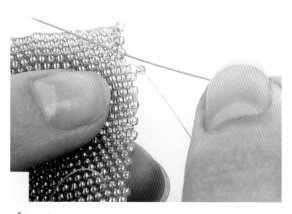

1 Pick up 52 beads and weave 39 rows of peyote stitch. The zigzag ends will be symmetrical.

2 Weave the needle through to emerge from a bead one row up and two beads in from the bottom right-hand corner.

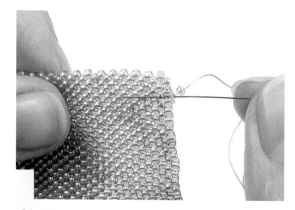

3 Pick up a sequin, then a seed bead. Skipping the bead, take the needle back through the sequin and through the same bead it emerged from.

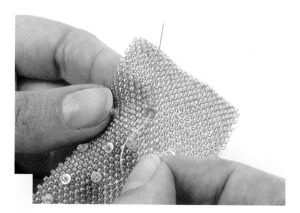

4 Weave the needle through to a few beads along and repeat the process. Add sequins across the beading, clustering them in the bottom right-hand corner and spacing them out further as you work up and across. Use the main photograph for guidance.

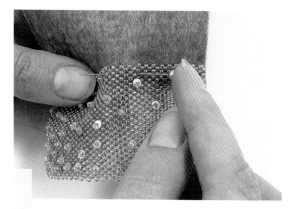

5 Lay the fabric flat and lay one zigzag edge of the beading over one short end, overlapping it by ¼ in (5mm). With one central pin, pin the beading to the fabric, sliding the pin between beads.

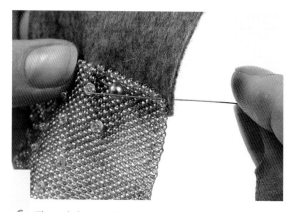

6 Thread the needle and make a knot in the end of the thread. From the back of the fabric, bring the needle through in line with the edge of the first protruding bead.

7 Take the needle through the bead then back down through the fabric, right next to the bead. Bring the needle up through the fabric beside the next protruding bead and repeat the process until the whole beaded edge is stitched to the fabric. Remove the pin after you have stitched a few beads as it will distort the edge, making it difficult to sew neatly; hold the pieces together as you stitch the rest of the seam.

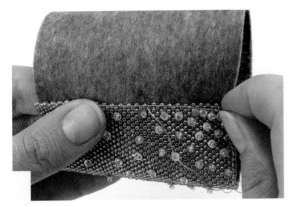

8 Repeat the process to attach the other side of the beading to the other edge of the fabric to make a tube.

9 Using the technique described in Step 3, add a few sequins to the fabric, to the left of the beading.

10 Fold the bead and fabric tube flat so that ¹⁄₂in (1cm) of fabric is at the front on the right-hand side. Using beaded blanket stitch (page 126), stitch across the bottom of the tube. When stitching across the beaded section, take the needle between the beads on the bottom row.

GETTING IT RIGHT
....

This case was made for a flat mirror compact measuring 3in (7.5cm) square. If you want to adjust the dimensions, follow these rules. The beaded panel measures the full height of the compact and approximately half the width. The felt rectangle measures the full height of the compact by twice the width, minus the width of the beaded panel, plus ¹⁄₂in (1cm) for the ¹⁄₄in (5mm) underlap on each side of the panel.

bead-embroidered motifs

There are many different ways of using beads in embroidery, and here are four of the easiest and most popular.

beaded flowers

This technique uses simple lazy daisy stitch to make tiny beaded flowers.

MATERIALS

· ·

40 variegated matte green delica
   beads (per flower)
1 variegated purple seed bead
   (per flower)
beading needle
purple beading thread

TECHNIQUES

· ·

lazy daisy, page 126

1 Work each flower using four lazy daisy stitches and ten green delica beads for each stitch.

2 Stitch a purple bead into the center of each flower to complete the motif.

bugle-beaded star

In this subtle motif, the type of bead used determines the shape of the design.

MATERIALS

16 pale blue delica beads
   (per star)
8 6mm pale blue bugle
   beads (per star)
beading needle
blue beading thread

TECHNIQUES

straight stitch, page 127

1 Bring the needle up through the fabric and pick up one delica, one bugle, and one delica and make a straight stitch. Bring the needle up through the fabric at the starting point and repeat the process three times more to make a cross.

2 Work one more straight stitch with the same sequence of beads between each arm of the cross to make a star.

freehand embroidery

Freehand embroidery doesn't have to be complex. Use a single stitch and type of bead, and embellish the pattern with sequins for a glamorous effect.

MATERIALS

size 9 pink seed beads
12mm lilac sequins
beading needle
green beading thread

TECHNIQUES

feather stitch, page 127

GETTING IT RIGHT

For an extra finishing touch, the buttons can be embellished, too, by stitching a sequin that is the same diameter over them.

1 Embroider freehand a wandering line of feather stitch with six pink beads on each stitch.

2 Embellish the embroidery with lilac sequins. Take the needle through the fabric to where you want the sequin to be. Pick up a sequin and pink bead and, skipping the bead, take the needle back down through the sequin.

heart motif

Outline shapes are easily embroidered onto almost any fabric.

MATERIALS

approximately 95 pale green
   delica beads
beading needle
green beading thread
template, see right
scissors
water-soluble fabric marker

TECHNIQUES

couching, page 125
backstitch, page 125

1 Enlarge the template to the required size and cut it out with scissors.

2 Lay the cutout on the fabric in the required position and draw around it with the fabric marker.

3 Using couching, embroider the design. Use backstitch to make any tight curves or detailed shapes.

4 Thread the needle with doubled thread and take it through all the beads in the design again, pulling gently to ensure that they sit neatly.

5 Use a dampened paper towel to remove any traces of the fabric marker.

brooch cushion

Rich color and luxurious texture complement the style of this plump little cushion.
As well as being a pretty item in its own right, keep this cushion sitting on your dressing
table to hold your brooches and pins easily to hand.

MATERIALS
• •

240 size 12 bronze seed beads
187 size 10 copper seed beads
1 size 6 gold bead
beading needle
brown beading thread
2 circles of burnt-orange velvet,
    5½-in (14-cm) in diameter
sewing needle
tacking thread
sewing machine
burnt-orange sewing thread
stuffing
1¼-in (29-mm) self-cover button
scrap of burnt-orange velvet

TECHNIQUES
• •

chain stitch, page 120

1 Work chain stitch with the first link being one
bronze seed, then one copper seed bead, repeated
six times. Subsequent links will be one bronze bead,
then one copper bead, repeated five times, then one
bronze bead. Following this pattern, make a chain
35 links long.

2 Using the working thread from the last link
of the chain, pick up one bronze bead, then one
copper bead, repeated twice, then one bronze bead.
Ensuring that the chain is not twisted, take the
needle through the halfway copper bead on the
first link in the chain.

3 Pick up the same pattern of beads as in Step 2 and take the needle back through the halfway copper bead on the other end of the chain to join it and make a circle. Weave in the ends of the threads.

4 Right-sides facing, tack the two velvet circles together. Taking a ⅝in (1.5cm) seam allowance, machine stitch around the edges, leaving a small gap. Stitch slowly and carefully, keeping the circle of stitching as round as possible.

5 Take out the tacking threads and turn the cushion right-side out. Stuff the cushion firmly.

6 Using the sewing thread, slip stitch the gap closed, keeping the seam circular.

7 Slip the beaded chain around the cushion, positioning it over the seam.

GETTING IT RIGHT
. . . .
Machining a perfect circle
is important here,
and the trick is to keep
the machine running at
a slow, constant speed
all around the circle—
not to sew a few stitches
at a time, then stop.

8 Using the sewing needle and thread, attach the chain to the seam. Secure the thread to the seam, then make a tiny backstitch over a point in the chain where two links join. Pull the thread tight so that it slips between the beads. Inside the cushion, push the needle along to the next joining point in the chain. Bring the needle out and make a backstitch over the beads, as before. Repeat until you have stitched right around the chain. Secure the thread with a few tiny stitches under the chain.

9 Following the steps for Rose Buttons on page 90, make a covered button. The central bead is copper, surrounded by a circle of five alternate copper and bronze beads. The outer circle is 19 bronze beads. Leave the edge of the button unbeaded.

10 Thread the sewing needle with sewing thread and double it. Push the needle through the centre of the cushion, from bottom to top, leaving a long tail of thread at the bottom. Thread on the button and stitch back down through the cushion.

11 Cut off the needle and pull the ends of the threads hard to pull the button down into the cushion. Knot the threads tightly and trim them short.

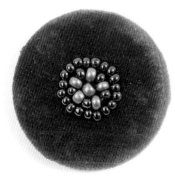

Above: If you change the sizes of the beads used to make the chain, experiment with different arrangements to decorate the button.

beaded bag

Perfect for a wedding or evening event, this delicate, sparkling bag can be made to complement your dress perfectly. Choose a fabric that matches and beads to co-ordinate or to pick up any accent colors. It isn't a difficult project to make, although it is more time-consuming than other items in this book.

MATERIALS

90 6mm pearl disc beads
204 size 8 pale pink hex beads
219 3mm pearl beads
1820 size 10 pale pink seed beads
28-gauge silver wire
wire cutters
beading needle
white beading thread
crimp beads
chain-nose pliers
7$\frac{1}{2}$ x 5$\frac{1}{2}$in (19 x 14cm) rectangle
    of ivory silk fabric

sewing machine
iron
ivory sewing thread
sewing needle

TECHNIQUES

wirework, page 124
simple fringe, page 121

1 Cut a 12-in (30-cm) length of wire. Thread on a bead pattern of one disc bead, one hex, one pearl, five seed, one pearl, then one hex, repeated 12 times.

2 Using pliers, twist the ends of the wire tightly together. Cut them short and hide them under the adjacent bead.

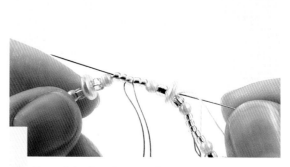

3 Cut twelve 24-in (60-cm) lengths of wire. Thread one length through every third seed bead on the beaded circle. Thread the length of wire halfway through, then bend it in half over the bead.

4 Thread the beading needle with a double length of white beading thread. Reinforce the beaded circle by taking the thread through all the beads on it. Tie the ends of the thread in a firm double knot and hide them under an adjacent bead.

5 Thread ten seed beads onto one end of each length of folded wire and ten seed beads and one pearl onto the other. Ensure that you thread onto alternate strands so that each bead-only strand has a bead-and-pearl strand next to it.

6 Thread the end of the bead-only strand through the pearl on the strand on the next folded length along. Repeat this to make a series of triangles around the beaded circle.

7 Thread one hex bead, one disc, one hex, then one pearl onto each pair of ends. Pull gently on the ends to ensure that all the beads are sitting tightly against one another.

8 Repeat Steps 5–7 six times more, threading ten seed beads onto one end of the wire protruding from a pearl, and ten seeds and a pearl onto the other end. Thread each bead-only strand through the pearl on the next strand along to form a trellis.

9 Repeat Steps 5–6 once more.

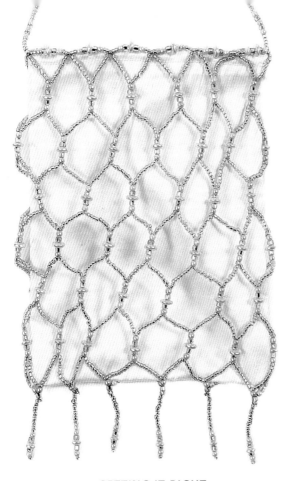

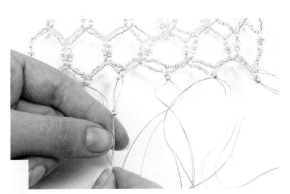

10 Press the beaded trellis flat, aligning the ends of wire on opposite sides. Thread all four ends of wire of each opposite pair through a hex bead.

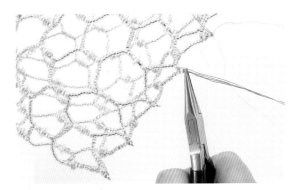

11 Thread all four ends of wire through a crimp bead. Squash the bead and cut the ends of the wires very short.

GETTING IT RIGHT

With so many ends of wire and loose beads, this project can be a bit fiddly. The trick is to work slowly and methodically in building up the repetitions, bending over each strand of wire once you have finished threading on a sequence of beads to prevent them falling off.

12 Thread the beading needle with a very long double length of thread and knot the ends around the wire above the first pearl in the last section of trellis on the right-hand side of the bag. Cut the ends of the threads short and pull gently on the needle to hide them under the pearl. Take the needle through the beads to emerge through the hex bead above the crimp on the right-hand side of the bag.

13 Pick up 15 seed beads, one pearl, one hex, one, disc, one hex, one pearl, then one seed. Skipping the last bead, take the needle back through the strand. Weave the needle through the trellis to the next hex bead along and repeat the process until every crimped end has a fringe.

14 Weave the needle through the trellis and tie the ends of the thread around the wire above a pearl bead to secure it. Use the point of the needle to push the knot under the bead to hide it.

15 Thread the beading needle with 47½in (120cm) of thread, double it, and knot the ends of the thread together. On one side of the bag, take the needle over the wire that forms the original circle and then through the loop formed by the knotted end. Pull the loop tight so that the knot slips between two beads and disappears.

16 Pick up a bead pattern of five seed beads, one pearl, one hex, one pearl, one hex, then one pearl, repeated nine times, followed by five seed beads.

17 Take the wire over the beaded circle on the other side of the bag and back through the strand of beads again to make a handle. Pull the beads up tight so that the thread disappears between the beads on the circle.

18 Tie the ends of thread together around the wire on the original side of the circle and hide the knot inside a bead.

19 Thread the needle with the ends of thread and take them back through the handle a little way before cutting them short.

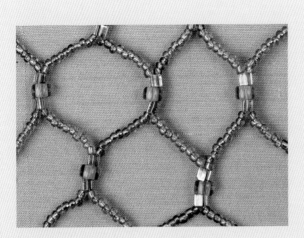

variation

Here, a cube bead, a large round feature bead, and another cube bead join the wire diamonds, and there are ten size-9 seed beads between every join. A blue silk bag complements the bright green beads.

variation

A color palette of black and silver produces a contemporary, sophisticated effect. A 10mm black bugle bead with a size-10 silver seed bead at each end connects the wire diamonds, and there are a further eight silver beads between the joins. A black net bag is good-looking, though quite fragile.

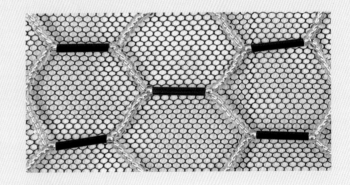

20 Fold the silk rectangle in half lengthwise. Taking a ¹⁄₂-in (1-cm) seam allowance, machine down each long side to make a bag. Turn the bag right-side out.

21 Wrong sides facing, turn under a ¹⁄₂-in (1-cm) double hem all around the top edge of the bag and machine it in place.

22 Slip the silk bag inside the beaded trellis. Thread the beading needle and stitch the two together around the top circle. Make a stitch through every second and fourth seed bead and every hex bead. Between the beads, slip the needle through the hem at the top of the silk bag.

rose buttons

All dressmakers know that the right buttons can make all the difference to the look of a garment. Making your own beaded buttons allows you to choose exactly the right colors to add decorative detail to the plainest shirt or dress. Either use the same fabric as the main garment, or choose something to complement or contrast.

MATERIALS

1 pale green delica bead
 (per button)
approximately 20 lavender delica
 beads (per button)
approximately 12 pink delica
 beads (per button)
fabric to match or complement
 the garment
embroidery hoop
compasses
beading needle
beading thread to match fabric
self-cover button

TECHNIQUES

bead embroidery, see page 125

GETTING IT RIGHT

As the ring of beads surrounding the button makes it larger, you must buy a smaller size of self-cover buttons than you would normally so that they will fit through the buttonholes of the garment. It is usually best not to machine-wash beaded buttons: either cut them off before washing, or check that the beads you have used can be laundered and hand-wash the garment.

1 Put the fabric into an embroidery hoop. Using the compasses, lightly draw a pencil circle the diameter recommended by the manufacturer to cover your button.

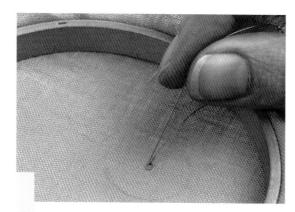

2 Bring the needle up through the fabric in the center of the circle. Thread on one green bead and take the needle down through the fabric, just to one side of where it came out.

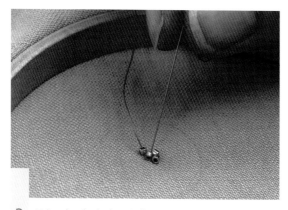

3 Using backstitch, stitch six lavender beads in a circle around the green bead.

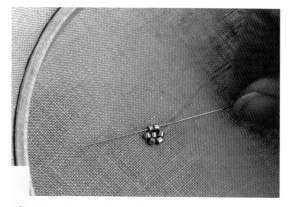

4 Bring the needle up through the fabric between two beads. Thread the needle through all of the lavender beads, take it back down through the fabric and gently pull the thread taut to make a tight, even circle of beads.

5 Again using backstitch, stitch 12 pink beads in a circle around the lavender ones. Thread the needle through all the pink beads and then pull the thread taut, as before. Secure the thread on the back of the fabric.

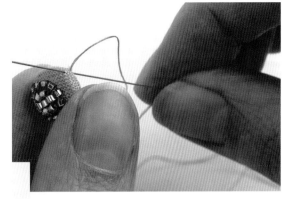

6 Cut out the circle of fabric with the beaded rose in the center. Following the manufacturer's instructions and using a long length of thread, work gathering stitches around the edge of the circle of fabric and cover the button. Do not cut the gathering thread and make sure that it hangs free when you snap the back onto the button.

7 Thread the needle with the free end of the gathering thread, then slip the needle between the fabric and button and bring it out on the edge of the button.

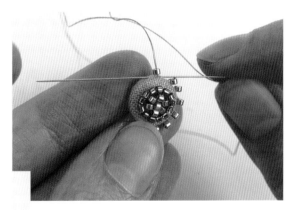

8 Using backstitch, and slipping the needle between the fabric and the button, stitch a ring of approximately 14 lavender beads around the edge of the button. Secure the thread with some tiny stitches in the fabric at the back of the button.

variation

This button was made using the same techniques as the rose button, but a simple heart motif was backstitched onto the fabric with pink delica beads.

chain belt

Formed from a simple repeat pattern, this contemporary belt is embellished with a beaded fringe and dangling ribbons. Here the belt is worn with a softly faded denim skirt—which the strong blue colors of the beads were chosen to complement—but it also looks fantastic with a simple shift dress.

MATERIALS

approximately 2500 size 11 dark
   blue seed beads
approximately 375 size 7 bright
   blue seed beads
beading needle
blue beading thread
2 20-in (50-cm) lengths of ⅛-in
   (3-mm) wide dark blue ribbon

TECHNIQUES

chain stitch, page 120
simple fringe, page 121

1 The first link of the chain is four seed beads followed by one size 7 bead, repeated four times. Subsequent links will be four seed beads followed by one size 7 bead, repeated three times, then followed by four seeds. Following this pattern, make a chain to fit around your hips.

2 Thread the needle and, starting at one end of the chain, weave it through to emerge after the lower size 7 bead on the first link.

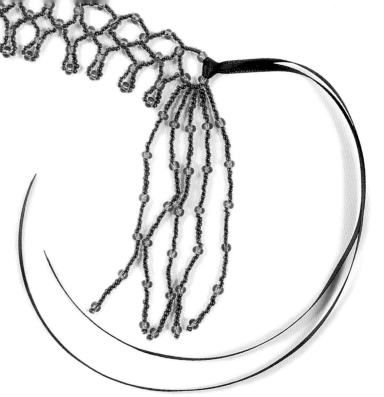

GETTING IT RIGHT
. . . .
This belt has 63 links and
measures 32in (80cm) in length.
To make one to fit you perfectly,
simply measure your hips and
make a chain with enough
links to fit that measurement.
The chain will stretch a little, so
check it around your hips before
starting the loops.

3 Thread on four seed beads, followed by one
size 7 bead, repeated twice, then followed by four
seed beads.

4 Take the needle back through the first size 7
bead on the string to form a loop.

5 Pick up four seed beads and take the needle
through the lower size 7 bead on the next link along
the chain. Repeat Steps 3–5 until you reach the end
of the chain.

6 Weave the needle through so that it emerges after
the end size 7 bead at one end of the chain. Make a
simple fringe of eight seed beads, followed by one
size 7 bead, repeated six times, then one seed bead.

7 Skipping the last bead, take the needle back up through the string, then through the next seed bead on the first circle of the chain.

8 Repeat the process four times more, so that one strand of fringe hangs between each bead on the bottom outer quarter of the link. Fringe the other end of the chain in the same way.

9 Trim the ends of the ribbon at an angle. Loop a length of ribbon in half and, from the front, thread the loop through the fringed link on one end of the chain. Tuck the cut ends through the loop and pull it tight. Attach the other length of ribbon to the other end of the chain in the same way. Fasten the belt around your hips by knotting the ribbons together.

variation

Fire-polished beads and size 11 seed beads strung in a similar pattern to the belt make a delicate bracelet. There are three seed beads between each fire-polished bead on the links, with a fire-polished bead and the seed bead on either side joining one link to the next. The loops have three seed beads before the first fire-polished bead and five either side of the second fire-polished bead, with another three joining the first fire-polished bead to the next link in the chain. The fastening ring and bar sit in the middle of a string of six seed beads that loops out from the beads either side of the fire-polished bead at each end of the bracelet.

lavender sachet

An ever-popular item in our lingerie drawers, lavender bags should be pretty as well as sweet-smelling. This quick-to-do version is made from organza ribbon and embellished with seed beads and a single feature bead. Instead of the feature bead, you could trim the neck of the bag with a scrap of complementary ribbon or a few bead fringes.

MATERIALS

approximately 90 size 12
   seed beads
beading thread
beading needle
9in (23cm) of 1½-in (4-cm) wide
   wire-edged organza ribbon
teaspoon
dried lavender
hanging heart bead

TECHNIQUES

bead embroidery, page 125

GETTING IT RIGHT

It isn't essential to use wired ribbon, but it does help to
create a ruffle that stands up at the top of the bag.

1 Fold under 1¼in (3cm) of each end of the
ribbon. Fold the ribbon in half lengthways, with the
folded-under ends inside and tops aligning perfectly.

2 Thread the needle and make a tiny knot in the
end of the thread. Starting at the open top, work
beaded blanket stitch down one side of the ribbon,
stitching through all layers of ribbon with each stitch,
so that the folded-under edges are stitched into the
seam. Make the stitches very tiny—the length of the
bead—and just catch the edges of the ribbon. Secure
the thread at the end of the stitching with a few tiny
stitches through the edge of the ribbon. Stitch the
other side of the ribbon in the same way.

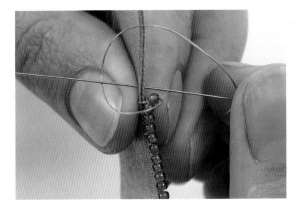

3 Using the teaspoon, fill
the bag with lavender to within
¾in (2cm) of the top. Pack the
lavender in tightly to create a
plump sachet.

4 Using the needle and thread,
gather the neck of the bag tightly
above the lavender. Bind the
thread around the gathers a few
times, then secure it with several
stitches through them.

5 Stitch the heart bead to the
gathered neck of the bag.

fringed stole

A stole is a wonderfully glamorous accessory that will add instant classic style to an evening outfit. The last thing it must be is skimpy, so this one is made from lots of rustling silk for a full, luxurious look. The bead-fringed ends are not only decorative, but will help the stole to drape beautifully over your shoulders and arms.

MATERIALS

3116 size 12 mauve glass seed beads with pink core

204 mauve glass cube beads with pink core

beading needle

pink beading thread

72in (180cm) of 43-in (110-cm) wide pale pink silk

two 11 x 6in (28 x 16cm) rectangles of pale pink silk

two 11 x 6in (28 x 16cm) rectangles of medium-weight iron-on interfacing

iron

sewing needle

basting thread

sewing machine

pale pink sewing thread

TECHNIQUES

simple fringe, page 121

1 Fold the large piece of silk in half widthways. Taking a ⅝-in (1.5 cm) seam, machine the two long selvedge edges together. Fold the fabric so the seam runs along the center back and press the seam open.

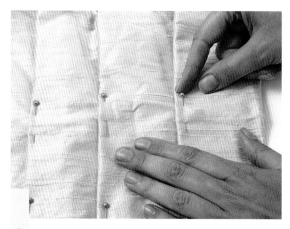

2 Turn the fabric tube right side out. At each short end, make three evenly spaced pleats to reduce the width to 9¾in (25cm). Pin the pleats in position.

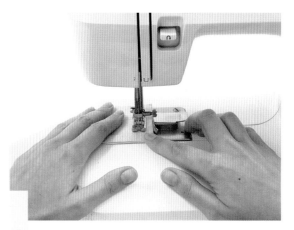

3 Iron a piece of interfacing onto the back of a rectangle of silk. Press under ½in (1cm) on each long edge of the rectangle. Right sides facing, fold the rectangle in half widthways, aligning the pressed-under edges perfectly.

4 Taking a ⅝-in (1.5-cm) seam allowance, machine stitch the short edges of the rectangle together. Turn it right side out and press it flat, ensuring that you press the bottom folded edge, too.

5 Thread the beading needle with a long length of beading thread and knot one end. From the inside, push the needle through the fabric, right in a bottom corner. Pick up one seed bead, one cube, 30 seeds, one cube, and one seed. Skipping the last bead, take the needle back up the string to make a simple fringe.

6 At the top of the string, push the needle back through the fabric as close as possible to where it came out. On the inside, slip a bead over the needle.

7 Skipping the bead, take the needle back down through the fabric, again in the same place, and through the first two beads on the string.

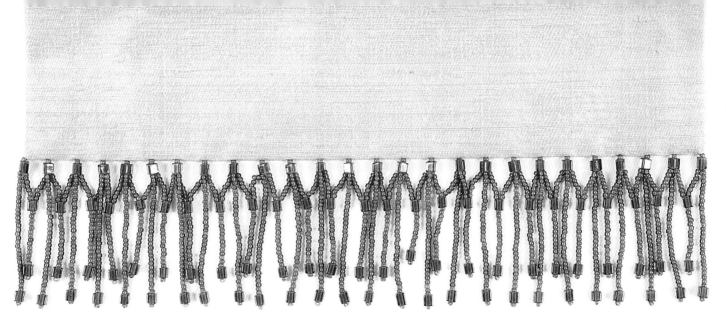

8 Pick up seven seed beads, one cube, 14 seeds, one cube and one seed. Skipping the last bead, take the needle back up the string to emerge after the first cube.

9 Pick up seven seed beads, one cube, and one seed, and take the needle through the fabric ½in (1cm) along the folded edge from the first string. Repeat Steps 6–7.

10 Pick up 30 seed beads, one cube, then one seed. Skipping the last bead, take the needle back up the string and through the fabric and the bead on the inside. Repeat Steps 7–10 until the whole edge is fringed.

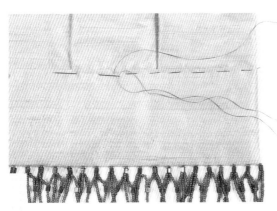

11 Slip the fringed end over the pleated end of the stole. Baste it in place along the top edge, ensuring that the top edges are directly opposite one another.

12 Machine stitch along the top edge, as close to the edge as possible, making sure you catch both edges in the stitching. Remove the basting thread. Use the remaining rectangle and beads to make a fringed end for the other end of the stole.

silk bag

This delicate drawstring bag, with a row of eyelets around the neck, can be made in almost any size and will have many uses. Keep it on your dressing table to hold jewelry, or use it as an evening bag. In a smaller size it will store a single piece of precious jewelry safely away from damage, or serve as an evening make-up bag.

MATERIALS

322 pale pea-green delica beads
129 bright pea-green glass
   seed beads
9 x 8³⁄₄in (23 x 22cm) piece of
   pale aqua dupion silk
9in (23cm) of ³⁄₄-in (2-cm) wide
   fusible webbing
iron
ruler
pencil

eyelet punch
weighted hammer
10 silver eyelets
eyelet setter
pale aqua sewing thread
sewing machine
beading needle
pale blue beading thread
pea-green stranded
   embroidery thread

TECHNIQUES

simple fringing, page 121

1 Turn down 1¹⁄₂in (4cm) along one long side of the silk and iron the fold. Lay the fusible webbing under the edge of the turn-down and iron it in place.

2 On the turn-down, 1¹⁄₄in (3cm) down from the folded edge, measure in 1¹⁄₈in (2.5cm) from the edge and make a tiny pencil mark. Make 9 more pencil marks at ³⁄₄in (2cm) intervals across the silk. Using the eyelet punch, punch a hole at every marked point.

3 Slip an eyelet into each hole and fix it in place with the eyelet setter.

4 Right-sides facing, fold the silk in half widthways. Machine stitch down the side and across the bottom of the rectangle, taking a 1/2in (1cm) seam. Clip the corners, turn the bag right side out, and press it.

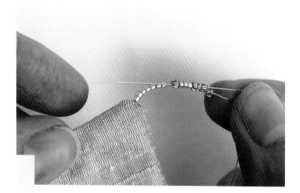

5 Thread the needle and knot the end. From the inside, bring the needle through a bottom corner. Pick up seven delica beads, one seed, three delica, and four seeds. Skipping the last bead, take the needle back through the string to emerge after the first seed bead.

6 Pick up seven delica beads. Take a tiny stitch through the pressed bottom edge of the bag, from front to back, 5/8in (1.5cm) along from where the needle came out. Repeat Steps 5–6 across the bottom of the bag.

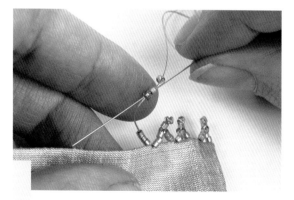

7 Starting at one corner, work similar fringing around the top edge of the bag. Pick up three delica, one seed, one delica, then one seed bead. Skipping the last bead, take the needle back down the strand to emerge after the first seed bead.

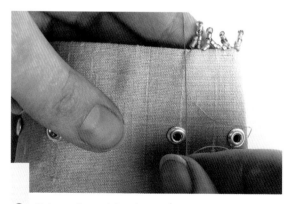

8 Pick up three delica beads. Take a tiny stitch from front to back through the edge of the fabric, as before, but 1/2in (1cm) along from where the needle came out. Repeat Steps 7–8 right around the top edge of the bag.

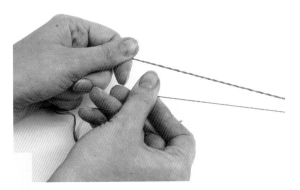

9 Cut three 20in (50cm) lengths of embroidery thread. Tie them together with a knot 2½in (6cm) from one end. Ask a friend to hold the knot, then divide the threads below it into two groups (one group of two threads and one single thread). Take a group in each hand and twist them in the same direction.

10 Twist until the threads start to coil up on themselves, then bring the ends together and, holding them firmly, ask your friend to let go of the knot. The threads will coil around themselves, making a cord. Tie the other ends together in a knot 2½in (6cm) from the end.

11 Thread the cord in and out of the eyelets around the top of the bag so that both ends emerge from the same eyelet.

12 Fray the ends of the threads below the knots. Thread a seed bead onto each strand and secure it by tying a double knot around it. Don't try to position the beads in exactly the same spot on the threads; the tassel will be more interesting if the beads are at different heights.

lipstick case

Gloriously glamorous, this beaded lipstick case has a retro feel that is brought up to date with vibrant color. The frog charm is more than just decorative—it's there to remind you that kissing frogs can, just sometimes, have great results.

MATERIALS

approximastely 260 size 9
    green seed beads
approximately 950 size 9
    pink seed beads
beading needle
green and pink beading
    threads
frog charm with hole
    drilled through the middle
glue spots

TECHNIQUES

peyote stitch, page 116

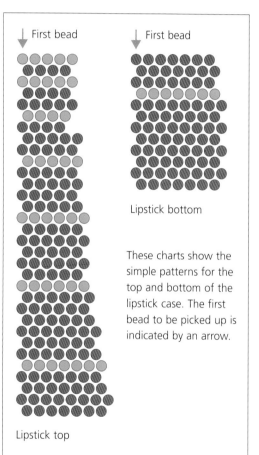

These charts show the simple patterns for the top and bottom of the lipstick case. The first bead to be picked up is indicated by an arrow.

Lipstick top

Lipstick bottom

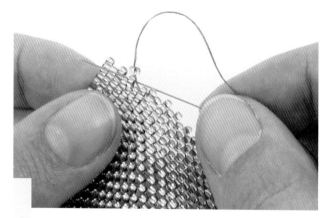

1 Thread the needle with green thread and pick up one green, one pink, one green, two pink, one green, three pink, one green, four pink, one green, five pink, one green, six pink, one green, four pink beads (see Getting It Right). Keeping the stripe pattern correct, work a strip of peyote stitch long enough to wrap snugly around the cover of your lipstick, ending with an even-number row so that the two zigzag ends will lock together.

GETTING IT RIGHT

This case was made to fit a lipstick with a cover measuring 2in (5cm) long and a base section measuring ¾in (2cm) long. If your lipstick is a different length, simply use enough beads to make strips of peyote that are each one bead longer than the cover and the base.

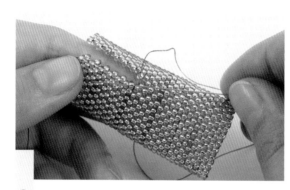

2 Join the ends of the peyote strip to make a tube. Slip the tube over the lipstick cover with the green edge at the top. Position it so that the green bead just protrudes beyond the top of the cover.

3 Weave the needle through to emerge from one of the edge beads at the top of the cover. Thread on enough beads to reach across the end of the cover to the opposite bead. Take the needle under the stitch loop next to the opposite bead.

4 Take the needle back through the string of beads and under the stitch loop next to the bead it came out of.

5 Bring the needle back through the next stitch loop along and repeat Steps 3–4 until you reach the edge of one side of the tube. Weave the needle back to the middle and repeat Steps 3–4 in the opposite direction.

6 Weave the needle through the strings of beads to emerge in the middle of the central one. Thread on the frog and a green bead. Take the needle down through the frog, then thread it the opposite way through the middle string. Weave the thread into the tube to secure it.

7 Pick up three pink, one green, and eight pink seed beads. Following Steps 1–5, make a cover for the base section of the lipstick, but using pink instead of green beads and pink thread to make the end.

8 If the beaded tubes slip a little on the lipstick, stick a glue spot to the end of the lipstick, then push the beaded tube down onto it to hold it in place.

WIREWORK

Pliers are necessary for wirework, and it is worth buying the right types as it will make the job easier. There are three styles of pliers used in this book.

Round-nosed pliers (right) have round jaws and are used for bending wire into loops and circles.

Chain-nose pliers (above) have round outer and flat inner jaws and are for twisting wire and squashing crimp beads.

Craft pliers (below left) have serrated jaws (useful for gripping a needle and pulling it through a tight bead) with a cutting edge at the bottom for cutting wire, although you can buy dedicated wire cutters.

28-gauge wire (left) is used throughout this book as it is pliable but not too thin. It is available in a range of colors.

Bead-stringing wire (above) is stiffer and works well for necklaces.

Crimp beads (left) are most commonly used with wire for attaching new lengths or finishing a string of beads.

OTHER EQUIPMENT

Embroidery hoops are available in different sizes and are essential when bead-embroidering onto thin fabric.

A bead loom offers a relatively quick way to make strips of beading. You are limited to a fairly narrow width, and weaving all the ends in can be a pain, but for some projects they are ideal.

A ruler is vital for measuring the gaps between fringing; don't be tempted to judge it by eye as the end result will look uneven.

FINDINGS

These are metal attachments that you can sew or stick to your beadwork to turn it into a piece of jewelry. *Top to bottom*: barrette; stick pin; brooch pin; two types of clasp; two types of earring, one in different sizes, and an earring back; jump rings.

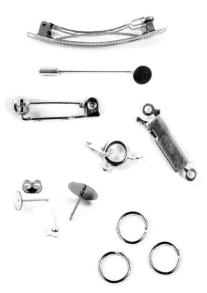

Beads

Each project in this book lists the beads by color and size, so it will be simple for you to buy what you need. Most beads are made from glass and come from Japan or the Czech Republic. Japanese beads tend to be machine produced and are very regular in size. This makes them good for needle- and loom-weaving as there are fewer irregular beads and thus less wastage. Czech beads often have a hand-made quality that adds character to beadwork, particularly bead embroidery.

Seed beads are circular with rounded tops and bases. They are available in a range of sizes, usually from size 5 to size 15—the bigger the number, the smaller the bead. Sizes 10, 11, and 12 are the most commonly used and are what most people mean when they refer to seed beads. The beads shown here are one color of glass.

Matte finish seed beads have been treated with acid to give them a flat colored surface.

Large seed beads are usually not available in such a wide range of colors and finishes as the small ones. The beads shown here are color-lined.

Color-lined seed beads have a colored core surrounded by glass. These beads have a clear glass outer layer and look good against the light.

These seed beads also have a colored core, but the glass surrounding them is a toning color. They offer a subtle color effect that works well when used in large quantities.

Delica or cylinder beads are tubular in shape. They are excellent for needle and loom weaving as they sit neatly against one another, producing a flat, even bead fabric. They also have a relatively large hole so thread can be passed through several times. Delicas are usually size 11.

Bugle beads are long cylindrical beads. Measured in millimeters, the most common lengths are 4mm, 6mm, and 9mm, but they can vary in width. Bugles can have a smooth or twisted finish and are good used in fringing.

Hex beads are also sometimes known as 2-cut beads. They are faceted and provide sparkle in a beaded project. They are usually sold by size, but sometimes by length in millimeters.

Fire-polished beads are faceted round beads that provide lots of sparkle. They offer a less expensive, but usually just as effective, alternative to crystal beads.

Buying and using beads

The quality of beads varies a lot and as a general rule you get what you pay for. It is usually better to buy good-quality beads as there will be fewer misshapen ones, thus less wastage and less time spent sorting them out. Do be aware that you shouldn't include irregular beads in your work. They will show particularly badly in needle- and loom-woven projects, although you can sometimes get away with them in fringing.

Beads are usually sold by weight in grams, although some retailers sell them by number. Surprisingly, the size or weight is not always marked on the packaging, so do ensure you are buying exactly what you need. The projects in this book give the quantity of beads needed to make them: an exact quantity if the project is one-size and an approximate quantity if you need to adjust the dimensions to fit. The chart on the right gives an approximate number of beads in a 5g package.

TYPE/SIZE OF BEAD	QUANTITY IN 5G PACKAGE
seed bead/6	120
seed bead/8	200
seed bead/9	300
seed bead/10	320
seed bead/11	450
seed bead/12	500
delica/11	800
hex/8	200
bugle/6mm	150
fire-polished beads	70

Starting work

There are two ways of starting a piece of beadwork, the first of which is probably easier if you are a beginner. Cut the longest piece of thread you can comfortably work with (I use 2yd/2m lengths) and thread a beading needle.

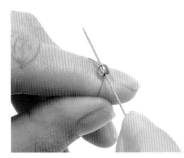

STOPPER BEADS

- A stopper bead provides a quick and simple way of starting beading.

- Pick up a bead that is a different color to the beads used in the project (so that you don't accidentally weave it in). Slide it down the thread to about 6in (15cm) from the end. Take the needle through the bead twice more.

- When taking the needle through the second and third times, hold the threaded bead tightly against your finger, holding it by the thread already going through it. This will help to prevent the needle splitting the thread as it passes through again. If you do split the thread, it can be difficult or impossible to unpick it later.

- As you work the first row of beading, you can loosen the threads through the stopper bead and slide it along the tail of thread to adjust the tension if necessary (see Tension, below).

- When you have finished the beadwork, use the point of the needle to unpick the thread from the stopper bead and weave it in (see Finishing and Starting Threads, below).

PEYOTE AND SQUARE STITCH

- If you are working peyote (as shown) or square stitch and the piece of beadwork is fairly narrow, you can tension the first rows on your fingers.

- Wrap the end of the thread several times around your left index finger, remembering that the tail must be 6in (15cm) long. (If you are left-handed, use your right index finger.) Thread on the required number of beads, then hold the thread below them between your thumb and second finger, as shown. Work the next row, keeping the thread taut between your fingers.

- This method can take a bit of getting used to, but I find it easier to produce perfect first rows this way.

FINISHING AND STARTING THREADS

I prefer not to use knots as they can work their way out from inside the bead they were hidden in, and they can come undone. I find it better to weave the ends of threads in. The only exceptions to this are the first loop of chain stitch (see page 120) and when attaching thread to wirework.

- End a piece of thread when there is about 6in (15cm) left. If you leave less than this, it becomes awkward to weave the end in securely.

- When weaving in ends, think about where beads may need to be added and avoid weaving in through any adjacent beads, or you may not be able to pass the needle through again to add the extra beads. For neatness, I like to leave long tails of thread at the beginning and end of a piece of beadwork and use these to do any joining or adding before weaving them in.

- To finish an end, take the needle through three beads in the next row. Bring it out between two beads and take it through three beads in the next row. Repeat this several times, changing direction. Cut the thread close to the beading.

- Start a new length of thread in the same way, weaving it into the existing beadwork and bringing it out through the same bead that the old thread emerged from.

TENSION

Getting the tension right can make all the difference to a piece of beading. If it is too loose, the work can be floppy with the beads loose within it, giving an untidy look. If too tight, the work can be inflexible, giving a stiff, awkward appearance. Over-tensioning can also result in breaking the thread, which means unpicking a section and starting it again.

Different stitches benefit from different tensions, and you will find tension notes for all the stitches in this section, plus notes on the projects where appropriate.

Generally, the trick is to pull gently and evenly on the thread: don't tug at it. Keep the tension even throughout the stitching and check at the end of every row that the beads are sitting correctly.

Peyote stitch

This is probably the most popular of the needle-weaving stitches. It is easy and quick to work and produces a flat bead fabric that is both decorative in itself and makes a good foundation for embellishment. One of the oddities of peyote stitch is that the beads picked up in Step 1 actually go on to form the first two rows, so read the steps carefully and look at the section on how to read a chart (see opposite) to make sure you understand the technique.

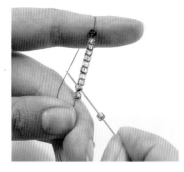

1 Place a stopper bead, then pick up the beads for the first two rows, ensuring it is an even number. If you are picking up enough beads to make a measured width (rather than a specified number) remember that because the rows are staggered the beading will not shrink when you work the next row. You must pick up the full width to start with. Pick up one more bead and, skipping the last bead on the string, take the needle through the next one. Pull gently on the thread so the new bead sits next to the last one on the string.

Most people find it easiest to work the first rows of peyote as shown, with the stopper bead at the top. This may cause confusion when you look at a chart, as the first bead to be picked up will usually be shown at the bottom. You just need to remember which way up you are working.

2 Pick up another bead and, skipping the next bead on the string, take the needle through the following one. Continue in this way until you reach the end of the row, with the needle going through the last bead. You have now worked three rows. Getting the first rows neat and even can take a little practice, but it is important to get them right or the rest of the work won't sit neatly.

3 Turn the work around so that the stopper bead is toward you. The zigzag pattern is obvious now and the rows will be quicker and easier to work. Pick up another bead and take the needle through the first protruding bead on the last row.

TENSION

Peyote is best worked with a fairly firm tension. Ensure that each bead slots neatly in between two protruding ones and that no beads are able to move around.

4 Continue adding beads between the protruding beads on the previous row until you have worked the required number of rows.

Peyote stitch swatch of 10 beads by 20 rows.

STRIPED PEYOTE

It's easy to work stripes in peyote without a chart. Simply pick up beads in the stripe pattern you want to use on the first string. As you add beads, it will be obvious which color they will sit next to, and so which color they should be.

Striped peyote stitch swatch of 10 beads by 20 rows.

JOINING PEYOTE

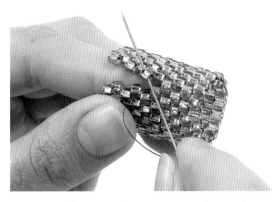

1 To turn a flat piece of peyote into a tube, work an even number of rows so the beads on the two zigzag ends "lock" together, with a protruding bead sitting next to an indented one. The swatch (below left) is an even number of rows, so you can see what the ends should look like.

Hold the ends together so that they "lock." The working thread will be coming out of an indented bead at the end of the last row. Take the needle through the opposite protruding bead on the other edge, then through the first protruding bead on the first side. Continue in this way, zigzagging the thread between protruding beads. When the seam is pulled up tight, it will be completely invisible. Weave in the end of the thread.

2 To join one edge of a tube to make a bag, flatten the tube so that the thread is coming out of a bead on one edge. Take the needle under the loop of thread that joins that bead to the one next to it. Then take the needle under the opposite loop of thread. Take the needle under the next loop of thread on the same side, then under the one opposite. Continue in this way until the whole edge is joined. Weave in the end of the thread.

READING A PEYOTE CHART

At first glance, a peyote chart may look very complicated, but it isn't really and once you start beading, it will make a lot more sense. However, do bear in mind that peyote charts are sometimes shown with the zigzag edges as the top and bottom, rather than the sides. It doesn't make any difference to the beading; you will always be starting at the bottom corner with the indented bead.

This chart (right) shows a peyote piece that is 10 beads tall by 20 rows wide. The first four rows of beads are numbered in the order in which they are picked up. In peyote stitch the rows are staggered, so adjacent beads actually belong to alternate rows. Here, the first row is outlined in green, the second in yellow, the third in mauve, and the fourth in pink.

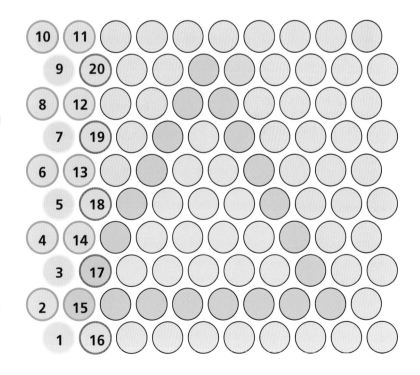

Brick stitch

This stitch looks very similar to peyote stitch, but the technique used to weave it is very different. Its great advantage over peyote stitch is that you can have an uneven number of beads in a row, which makes it more suitable for patterns that require a single central bead. It's also useful for working very tiny items. Rows are counted down the fabric rather than diagonally, as with peyote.

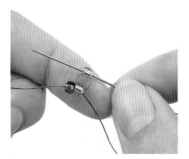

1 Place a stopper bead, then pick up the first two beads of the first row. Take the needle through both beads again, forming a loop of thread with a bead on each side. Pull the thread up tight so that the beads sit next to one another.

2 Pick up the third bead in the row. Take the needle up through the second bead and down through the third bead again to join it onto the row. Continue adding beads in this way—picking up the new bead and taking the needle up or down through the previous bead as appropriate, then through the new bead again—until you reach the end of the row. Don't worry if the first row looks a little uneven, it will straighten out a lot when the second row is added.

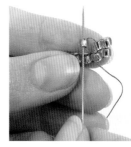

3 To start the second row, pick up the first two beads. Take the needle under the loop of thread that joins the last two beads on the first row.

4 Pull the thread through so that the new beads sit against the first row. Take the needle up through the second of the two beads just added and pull the thread tight.

5 Pick up the next bead, take the needle under the loop of thread joining the next two beads in the first row, then back through the bead just added. Continue adding beads in this way until you reach the end of the row.

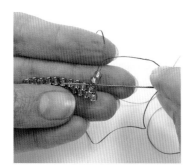

6 To start the next row, add on two beads following Steps 3–4.

TENSION

The first row of brick stitch needs to be worked tightly or subsequent rows will be very loose. If you have difficulty making the first row sufficiently stable, try looping the thread twice through each new bead. This will help to hold them close together without moving about. Subsequent rows should be worked with an even tension.

Brick stitch swatch of 10 beads by 10 rows.

Square stitch

This stitch looks very like loom weaving, but has the advantage of not having to weave in lots of ends of thread. The needle has to pass through each bead several times, so it's best suited for beads with reasonable-size holes. If you want to work with tiny beads, consider using a loom or use a finer needle and thread (see Equipment, page 112).

1 Place a stopper bead, then pick up the beads for the first row. Pick up the first bead of the second row and take the needle back through the last bead of the first row.

2 Take the needle back through the first bead of the second row once again.

3 Pick up the second bead of the second row. Take the needle through the second bead of the first row, then through the second bead of the second row again. Continue in this way, matching each bead to its counterpart in the first row, until you reach the end of the row.

4 The beads may well look rather wobbly in their rows. To stabilize them, take the needle through all the beads on the first row, then through all the beads on the second row, emerging in the correct position to start the third row.

5 Continue adding rows of beads in the same way. Stabilize each row by taking the needle through the previous one and the new one before starting the next row.

Square stitch swatch of 10 beads by 10 rows.

TENSION

This stitch is possibly the hardest to tension correctly. It is intended to produce a flexible fabric so is best worked with an even, but not tight tension. Pulling the thread hard distorts the beaded fabric and makes it uneven and inflexible.

INCREASING

When you reach the end of a row and have stabilized it (see Step 4, above), pick up two beads. Take the needle up through the first bead then down through the second. Ease the beads down so that the first bead sits at the end of the row you have just completed and the second bead is at the start of the next row.

Note that you cannot increase on just one row; an increase affects both the row you have just finished and the next one.

DECREASING

End of a row: finish one bead short. Stabilize the rows, but take the needle into the previous row one bead down from the end to prevent thread showing at the side of the last bead. Work the next row from the new row end position.

Start of a row: when stabilizing the previous row, simply bring the needle out one bead before the end of the row and work the next row from there.

You can decrease at the end of one row and at the start of the next, so a decease can affect just one row.

Chain stitch

This is the simplest of stitches and produces a row of linked circles. It can be worked with any size of bead and with different numbers of beads to make larger and smaller links.

1 Pick up the beads for the first link and slide them down the thread to 6in (15cm) from the end. Take the needle back through all of the beads.

2 Pull on both ends of the thread to form the beads into a tight circle. Tie the ends in a firm double knot, but do not cut either of them. When the chain is finished, weave the tail end into it.

3 Take the needle through the circle of beads to emerge after the bead that is opposite the starting point, or to the position stated in the pattern. Pick up the beads for the second link and take the needle back through the bead on the first link that the thread is coming out of. (As the two links share one bead, the number of beads for the second, and all subsequent links, will be one less than for the first link.)

TENSION

A beaded chain will never have perfectly round links, but to make the links as even and round as possible, this stitch is best worked with a very firm tension. If you are using a lot of small beads, rather than a mixture of sizes, you may find it better to take the needle through the whole link again before moving onto the next one. This will help to stiffen the circle and make it rounder.

Chain stitch swatch with 12 beads on the first link and 11 on the others.

4 Take the needle around the link in the same direction it was traveling in, to emerge after the opposite bead. Repeat Steps 3–4 until the chain is the required length.

Circles and loops

These are worked almost identically, but produce a different effect. As well as being a more oval shape, loops swing more freely than circles. Do check the pattern you are following to see if a circle or loop is needed, as the wrong element can make more difference than you might imagine.

Circle and loop together

To make a circle, pick up the required number of beads. Take the needle through the appropriate bead in the same direction it originally went through. Pick up more beads as needed.

To make a loop, pick up the required number of beads. Take the needle through the appropriate bead in the opposite direction to the one it went through originally. Pick up more beads as needed.

Simple fringe

Beaded fringes always look lovely; they are almost infinite in variety and add movement and sparkle to flat beadwork. These instructions are for the most basic type of fringe, but all fringes follow the same general principle.

1 Bring the needle out through the bead you want the fringe to start from and take it under the loop of thread that joins that bead to the next one along. Pick up the required number of beads and, skipping the last bead, take the needle back through the string.

TENSION

Fringing needs to be worked with a light tension or it will poke out stiffly and not swing.

2 Take the needle under the same loop of thread, then through the next loop along. Repeat the process until you have made the whole fringe. (Taking the needle under the stitch loops rather than through the beads allows the fringing to swing more freely. There are some exceptions to this in certain projects where you should follow the specific instructions given.)

Fringing hanging from a loom-woven strip.

Attaching findings

There is a wide variety of findings available and they fall into two main groups: those that are glued on and those that are stitched on.

You can buy special adhesives for gluing beads to metal, but I always use an epoxy adhesive that is suitable for the task. Do not use a runny adhesive or it will seep through the beads and spoil your work. Similarly, ensure that the adhesive you use dries clear or it may show. Follow the manufacturer's instructions carefully and always leave the item to dry for the stated length of time.

Findings that are stitched on are easy to use and all follow the same basic principle. For the sake of neatness, I like to use the tail ends of thread left from working the beadwork to attach the finding. Some people like to use a new length of thread however, because if you decide at a later date to change the finding, you can cut it off without any risk of the beadwork unraveling.

Thread the needle with the tail of thread and weave it through to emerge from the bead you want the finding to be attached to. Take the needle through the finding and back through the bead as many times as it will go through. Weave the end into the beadwork in the usual way.

A ring fastening attached to a loom-woven strip.

Loom weaving

Beading on a loom is the fastest way to create flat strips of beadwork, but there are some drawbacks. Setting the loom up and weaving in the ends when you've finished is time-consuming and can be fiddly, and the width of the loom restricts the size of the strip you can make.

In loom weaving the warp threads are those that are actually on the loom, while the weft threads are those that carry the beads. You will need one more warp thread than there are beads across the strip. Different types of bead loom are set up in different ways, but the basic principle is the same. Here are instructions for the most common type of loom, but do check the instructions supplied with your loom in case they vary.

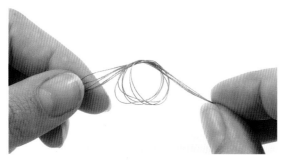

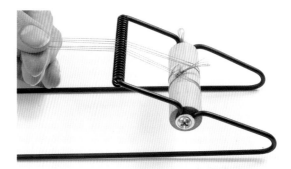

1 Work out the number of warp threads needed: here, there are five beads in each row, so six threads are needed. Add 20in (50cm) to the measured length of the finished project to allow for setting up the loom and weaving in the threads. Cut the number of threads you need and tie one end of them together with an overhand knot.

2 Divide the threads into two groups and loop the knot over the tack in one of the rollers. Wind the roller round so that most of thread is wound onto it with just enough left to reach to opposite roller, then tighten the nut on the roller to stop it moving further. Position the threads so that they sit in adjacent coils in the spring above the roller.

3 Lay the threads along the loom and position them in the coils on the spring at the other end of the loom. They must lie in straight, parallel lines. Use a needle to help you position them.

4 Tie the other thread ends together, as in Step 1. Loop the knot over the tack in the roller, as in Step 2. Loosen the roller nuts, wind 8in (20cm) of thread onto the second roller, then tighten both nuts. Start weaving from this end.

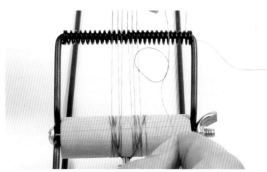

5 Thread a beading needle with 2 yards (2m) of thread. Leaving a 6in (15cm) tail, tie the end of the thread to an outer warp thread between the spring and the roller. (Some people prefer to tie the thread on above the spring so that it sits at the edge of the first row of beading. I prefer to do it as described, then use the point of the needle to unpick the knot and weave the end in later. This is a little more fiddly, but I worry that the knot might otherwise show.)

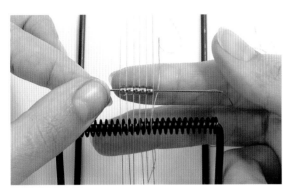

6 Pick up the beads for the first row and, keeping them on the needle, hold them under the warp threads. Use your free index finger to push them up so that one bead sits between each thread. Pull the needle through.

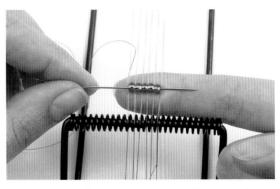

7 Keeping your finger in the same position, push the needle back through the beads, but going over the warp threads this time.

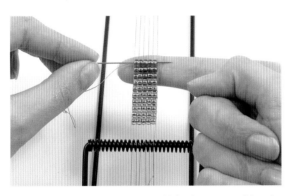

8 Simply repeat Steps 5–6 to add further rows of beads, as required.

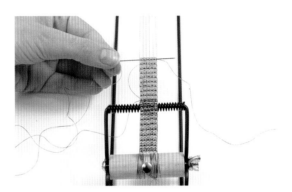

9 When the beading becomes too long to fit on the loom, loosen the rollers and wind the beading back. When you have about 6in (15cm) of thread left, take it off the needle and leave it hanging. Weave a new thread through three or four rows of the existing beadwork, bringing it out through the same bead as the old thread.

10 When you have finished beading, loosen the rollers and take the work off the loom. Cut the threads just above the overhand knots. Thread each one in turn into a needle and weave it into the beading. This can be difficult if the beads have very small holes, in which case it is best to weave different threads through one or two beads in each row rather than through whole rows. Weave in the ends of any threads at the sides of the work in the same way.

A loom-woven strip of 5 beads by 20 rows.

TENSION

Bead loom work should be worked with a light tension to keep it flexible and the outer edges even.

Wirework

Two types of wire are used in this book: 28-gauge wire and bead-stringing wire. 28-gauge wire is soft and pliable and is used for projects that need to be molded to a specific shape. Bead-stringing wire is stiff and springy and works well for necklaces and bracelets. Illustrated here are the techniques for securing both types of wire.

28-GAUGE WIRE

The most important thing with this wire is not to treat it roughly. If you twist too hard or bend it at the same point too often, it will break.

1 To join two ends of wire, grip them close to the beads with chain-nose pliers. Twist the ends around one another very tightly two or three times. The beads need to butt tightly together with the twist almost invisible between two of them. It can take a couple of attempts to get this right, so practice before starting a project.

2 Thread one end of the wire through several beads, Do the same with the other end, but in the other direction.

3 Using wire cutters, cut the ends of the wire as close as possible to the beads. If a short end sticks out, you can use the tip of a needle to tuck it under a bead. When finished, you shouldn't be able to see the join.

BEAD-STRINGING WIRE

Bead-stringing wire cannot be twisted, so you need to crimp the ends to secure them. Crimps can also be used on 28-gauge wire, but don't squash the crimp bead too hard or it can cut through the wire.

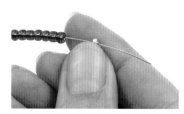

1 Slide a crimp bead onto the end of the beaded wire.

2 Using chain-nose pliers, squash the crimp bead. Squeeze the pliers as hard as you can to ensure that the bead is clamped tightly around the wire.

3 Using wire cutters, cut the end of the wire as close as possible to the crimp bead. Be aware that the end of the wire can be sharp, so this technique is not suitable for jewelry for children.

Embroidery stitches

A lot of embroidery stitches can be used with beads, so do experiment with stitches you like. Illustrated here are some of the most successful and popular bead embroidery stitches. They have been worked on wool felt, but can be stitched equally well on other fabrics in an embroidery hoop.

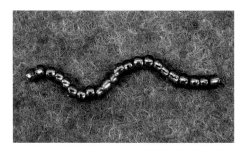

BACKSTITCH

This is an easy and versatile stitch to work and is suitable for making small, detailed motifs as it can be worked around tight corners. The trick is to keep the beads as close together as possible.

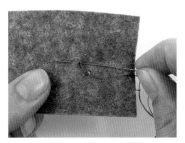

1 Thread the needle and knot the end. Bring the needle through the fabric from the back. Pick up a bead and make a backstitch through the fabric, putting the needle in the width of the bead from where it came out and bringing it out the same distance away.

2 Pull the thread through so that the bead is tight against the fabric and repeat the process, putting the needle into the fabric as close as possible to the first bead.

3 When you have finished backstitching the shape, take the needle through all of the beads. This helps to tighten and align them. Don't pull the thread too tight or you will pucker the fabric.

COUCHING

This simple stitch is ideal for making long, straight lines or gently curving lines. You need to use two threaded needles to make it.

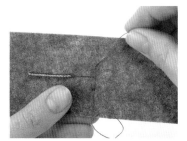

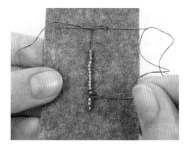

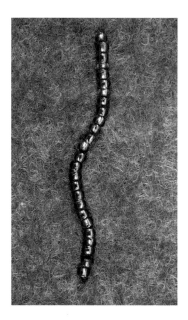

1 Knot the ends of both threads. From the back, bring one needle through the fabric where you want to start stitching. Thread on up to 20 beads (more than this can be difficult to handle). Slip the needle into the fabric to keep it out of the way. If couching a straight line, you can wind the thread around the needle to keep it taut.

2 Bring the second needle through the fabric between the third and fourth beads. Nudge the fourth bead up the thread. Take a tiny stitch over the thread, very close to the third bead, and back down through the fabric. Push the beads down against the stitch. Bring the needle through three beads further along and repeat until all the beads are attached. Pick up more beads on the first needle as necessary.

BLANKET STITCH

This stitch is brilliant for edging fabric or for sewing two edges together. It is also quick and easy to work, but do keep the stitches evenly spaced.

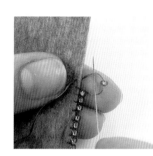

1 Pick up a bead and from back to front, bring the needle through the fabric.

2 Pull the thread through to form a small loop with the bead on it. Take the needle through the loop below the bead and pull the loop tight. Repeat the process until you have completed the stitching.

LAZY DAISY STITCH

This pretty stitch works well with small beads, but not with large ones. Don't put too many beads on each petal or they will droop and not keep their shape.

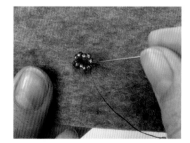

1 Thread the needle and knot the end. From the back, bring the needle out in the center of where you want the flower to be. Pick up the required number of beads and take the needle back down through the fabric exactly where it came out.

2 Pull the loop of beads up. Bring the needle up through the fabric at the opposite end of the loop and make a tiny stitch over it, pulling the thread tight so that the stitch slips between the beads and disappears. Repeat the process to make all the petals. Use a single stitch to put a contrasting color bead into the center of the flower.

FEATHER STITCH

Simple to work and decorative in effect, this stitch is excellent for freehand patterns.

1 Thread the needle and knot the end. From the back, bring the needle through the fabric where you want to start stitching. Pick up the required number of beads, then take the needle down again a little to the right of where it came out.

2 Pull the beads up and bring the needle back up in the middle of the curve, just above the thread.

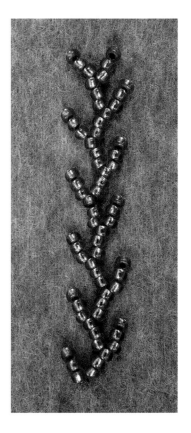

3 Pick up the same number of beads and take the needle down a little to the right again.

4 Repeat the process, taking the needle down to the left and right alternately.

STRAIGHT STITCH

This is a useful stitch for making simple patterns or for filling in the middle of a motif. Don't put too many small beads on a single stitch or it will droop.

1 Thread the needle and knot the end. From the back, bring the needle through the fabric where you want the first stitch to start. Pick up the required number of beads and slide them down the thread. Lay the beads flat on the fabric and take the needle back down as close as possible to the last bead. Repeat the process until you have completed stitching.

Suppliers

UK
The Spellbound Bead Company
45 Tamworth Street
Lichfield
Staffordshire WS13 6JW
tel: 01543 417650
www.spellboundbead.co.uk

The London Bead Co
339 Kentish Town Road
London NW5 2TJ
tel: 0870 203 2323
www.londonbeadco.co.uk

Ells & Farrier
20 Beak Street
London W1F 9RE
tel: 020 7629 9964

Creative Beadcraft Limited
(mail order branch of Ells & Farrier)
tel: 01494 778818
www.creativebeadcraft.co.uk

The Bead Shop
21a Tower Street
London WC2H 9NS
tel: 020 7240 0931
www.beadworks.co.uk

Whichcraft
13 Crookes Road
Broomhill
Sheffield S10 5BA
tel: 0114 266 1714
www.whichcraft.info

USA
Toho Shoji (New York) Inc
990 Sixth Avenue
New York
NY 10018
tel: 212 868 7465
www.toho-shoji.com

M&J Trimmings
1008 Sixth Avenue
New York
NY 10018
tel: 212 391 9072
www.mjtrim.com

New York Beads Inc
1026 Sixth Avenue
New York
NY 10018
tel: 212 382 2994

Index